SEPARATION OF POWERS

The MIT Press's publishing mission benefits from the generosity of our donors, including Mike Dornbrook.

SEPARATION OF POWERS

HOW TO PRESERVE LIBERTY IN TROUBLED TIMES

CASS R. SUNSTEIN

The MIT Press
Cambridge, Massachusetts
London, England

The MIT Press
Massachusetts Institute of Technology
77 Massachusetts Avenue
Cambridge, MA 02139
mitpress.mit.edu

The MIT Press would like to thank the anonymous peer reviewers who provided comments on drafts of this book. The generous work of academic experts is essential for establishing the authority and quality of our publications. We acknowledge with gratitude the contributions of these otherwise uncredited readers.

This book was set in ITC Stone Serif Std and ITC Stone Sans Std by New Best-set Typesetters Ltd. Printed and bound in the United States of America.

Library of Congress Cataloging-in-Publication Data is available.

ISBN: 978-0-262-05177-4

10 9 8 7 6 5 4 3 2 1

EU Authorised Representative: Easy Access System Europe, Mustamäe tee 50, 10621 Tallinn, Estonia | Email: gpsr.requests@easproject.com

The accumulation of all powers, legislative, executive, and judiciary, in the same hands, whether of one, a few, or many, and whether hereditary, self-appointed, or elective, may justly be pronounced the very definition of tyranny. Were the federal Constitution, therefore, really chargeable with this accumulation of power, or with a mixture of powers, having a dangerous tendency to such an accumulation, no further arguments would be necessary to inspire a universal reprobation of the system.

—James Madison

CONTENTS

1   FREEDOM AND TYRANNY   1

2   WHAT THE LEGISLATURE CANNOT DO   7

3   WHAT THE EXECUTIVE CANNOT DO   17

4   WHAT THE COURTS CANNOT DO   23

5   THE PRESIDENT'S IMMUNITY   27

6   THE MOST DANGEROUS BRANCH   37

7   DELIBERATIVE DEMOCRACY IN THE TRENCHES   49

8   THE GRAND NARRATIVE   59

9   NONDELEGATION CANONS   77

10 THE MAJOR QUESTIONS DOCTRINE   85

11 ARMS CONTROL IS HARD   95

12 PARTYISM   113

    EPILOGUE   127

ACKNOWLEDGMENTS   129
NOTES   131
INDEX   157

1 FREEDOM AND TYRANNY

It is March 27, 1933. Here is a headline in the *New York Times*: "Hitler Is Supreme Under Enabling Act."[1] Under that headline: "Chancellor, Preeminent Over Cabinet, Is Now Practically the German Government."[2] A few lines later, under that: "All Legislative Powers Have Been Transferred to Regime, Free to Refashion National Life."[3]

How might that transfer of powers, making the chancellor "free to refashion national life," be justified? Is there a theory? To say the least, that is a complicated question, but for a glimpse, turn to the justification by the Nazi legal theorist Carl Schmitt[4] of what happened in Germany on June 30, 1934.

That was the Night of the Long Knives,[5] in which Hitler ordered his elite guards to murder hundreds of people, including the leaders of the paramilitary Sturmabteilung (SA). The separation of powers was Schmitt's central target. He announced, "The real Führer is always a judge. Out of Führerdom flows judgeship."[6] Schmitt added, "One who wants to separate the two from each other or puts them in opposition to each other would have the judge be either the leader of the opposition or the tool of the opposition and is trying to unhinge the state with the help of the judiciary."[7]

It is worth pausing over this claim: "Out of Führerdom flows judgeship." Separation between leadership and judgeship creates a "leader of the opposition," and it unhinges the state. (*Unhinges* is an interesting term. What is the "hinge" here?) Schmitt insisted that it "was characteristic of the blindness about justice of the liberal way of thinking about law that it sought to make out of criminal law a great liberating charter, the 'Magna Carta of the criminal.'"[8] So much for "the liberal way of thinking about law." In Schmitt's view, "the Führer's action was true judging. It is not subject to law but is in itself the highest justice." This is a horror movie, but it is also real, and what was being said in the 1930s can be found, in various forms, today.

The US Constitution, an emphatically liberal document, is meant to protect freedom and to prevent tyranny. It is designed to "secure the Blessings of Liberty to ourselves and our Posterity."[9] And what are those blessings? Consistent with a prominent strand in liberal thought, we should take them to include a private realm of immunity from the power of the government—a realm in which people need not worry about being killed or being jailed or being subject to any kind of public coercion.[10]

Freedom from fear is a central goal of the system of separation of powers.

On one view, the separation of powers essentially *is* a bill of rights. The private realm of immunity certainly includes freedom of speech, freedom of religion, and protection of private property against takings without just compensation. In fact, it extends far more broadly. It includes a private sphere of freedom from official incursion.[11] It includes the rule of law, which is easily taken to include an independent judiciary and so to unhinge the state *on principle*. Whatever their precise content, the blessings of liberty allow people to be something like sovereigns over their own lives. The separation of powers is a way to secure those blessings. Hitler was of course an extreme case, and so was Stalin—but every era has its own extreme cases.

As the Constitution was designed, the blessings of liberty were even broader than that. They included the right to republican self-government.[12] The founding generation rejected the monarchical heritage, and so it abolished titles of nobility. It insisted on a principle of equality, which entailed at least a kind of popular sovereignty.[13] Adverting to the founding, Abraham Lincoln said this in 1854: "If the negro *is* a man, is it not to that extent, a total destruction of self-government, to say that he too shall not govern *himself*? When the white man governs himself that is self-government; but when he governs himself, and also governs *another* man, that is *more* than self-government—that is despotism. . . . No man is good enough to govern another man, *without that other's consent*. I say this is the leading principle—the sheet anchor of American republicanism."[14] In a few daring sentences, Lincoln connected the antislavery movement, calling for a right to self-government in individual lives, with the right to self-government in politics. Liberty was central to both domains. Lincoln was keenly aware that, consistent with the founding conception of republicanism, the Constitution and its system of separation of powers aimed to create a *deliberative democracy*—one that combined accountability with reason-giving in the public domain.[15]

In a deliberative democracy, the people certainly rule, in the sense that they control the operations of the government. But in a deliberative democracy, institutions are designed to increase the likelihood that decisions would be based not on the will of one person, but on the force of the better argument. Public power is not supposed to be exercised only on the ground that those in a position of authority think that it should be so exercised. They must justify themselves.[16] This too is a prominent part of the liberal tradition, and it is crucial to the separation of powers. It is a barrier to authoritarianism.

SIX, NOT ONE

Self-government is opposed to authoritarianism and tyranny, but it cannot come simply from voting. After all, Hitler was elected (by a plurality, but still). Consider in this light, and read anew, a famous sentence from James Madison: "The accumulation of all powers, legislative, executive, and judiciary, in the same hands, whether of one, a few, or many, and whether hereditary, self-appointed, or elective, may justly be pronounced the very definition of tyranny."[17] On its face, the Constitution aims to forbid the accumulation of all powers in the same hands. Of course, the idea of a king was foremost in the minds of those who fought the American Revolution and devised the founding document. But the separation of powers extends far beyond the rejection of the idea of kings.

Article I, section 1 of the Constitution says this: "All legislative Powers herein granted shall be vested in a Congress of the United States, which shall consist of a Senate and House of Representatives."[18] Article II, section 1 of the Constitution says this: "The executive Power shall be vested in a President of the United States of America."[19] Article III, section 1 of the Constitution says this: "The judicial Power of the United States shall be vested in one supreme Court, and in such inferior Courts as the Congress may from time to time ordain and establish."[20]

These provisions establish the separation of powers. (So much for Carl Schmitt.) We might want to emphasize the word *all* in Article I and the word *the* in Articles II and III. The Constitution seems to contemplate that there is something called *the* executive power and something called *the* judicial power, and that they are vested in particular institutions. And if *all* legislative powers are vested in Congress, then they would seem to be vested nowhere else.

The separation of powers, it is called, but we should immediately be able to see that the term is too broad and undifferentiated. In a way, it is a misnomer. The separation of powers is a *they*, not an *it*. It is an umbrella concept, and it seems to include six separations of powers:

1. The legislature may not exercise the executive power.
2. The legislature may not exercise the judicial power.
3. The executive may not exercise the legislative power.
4. The executive may not exercise the judicial power.
5. The judiciary may not exercise the legislative power.
6. The judiciary may not exercise the executive power.

The six separations can be taken to include three sets of prohibitions. There are two things that the legislature cannot do, two things that the executive branch cannot do, and two things that the judiciary cannot do. To get ahead of the game, my favorite is separation 3, and my second favorite is separation 4. But they are all important, and they are all terrific.

FUSSING

Still, let's fuss a little: The six propositions are mere inferences. My topic is separation of powers, not constitutional interpretation, and so I am not going to spend a lot of time on the question of how to interpret the Constitution.[21] But to understand the US Constitution, or any other constitution, we will have to say a few things about that topic.

The six propositions are not semantically mandated by the constitutional text. You can be a textualist without thinking that the Constitution requires them. The vesting of some power in some institution does not *necessarily* mean that some other institution may not exercise that power. But if we want to be faithful to the text, the relevant inferences are certainly plausible, and perhaps more than that. From the vesting of "all legislative powers" (herein granted) in Congress, we might well be inclined to infer that the executive and the judiciary do not have, and may not exercise, legislative powers. From the vesting of "the executive power" in the president, we might infer that Congress and the judiciary do not have, and may not exercise, executive power. From the vesting of "the judicial power" in federal courts, we might infer that Congress and the executive do not have, and may not exercise, judicial power.

Some of these inferences may not be entirely secure. It would be possible, for example, to agree that Article III vests the judicial power in courts, but also to insist that the executive may sometimes exercise some judicial power.[22] The text is not without ambiguity. Still, the inferences seem plenty reasonable. If *all* legislative powers are vested in Congress, it would be puzzling to say that the executive may exercise some such powers. At least as a textual matter, then, we might be inclined to endorse the six propositions.

Some people are *public meaning originalists*. Acknowledging that the text is not always clear (and not always close to clear), they nonetheless urge that the Constitution must be interpreted consistently with its original public meaning—that is, its meaning to the public at the time it was ratified. Perhaps the original public meaning of *the executive power* is full of surprises. Perhaps it means that the president can impound funds appropriated by Congress. Perhaps it does not mean that at all. Perhaps it means that the president has emergency power. Perhaps it does not mean that at all.

Public meaning originalists would want to consult history and to understand the separation(s) of powers in terms of the original public meaning,[23] and a careful historical investigation might tell us things that we do not expect and do not like.[24] Perhaps one or more of the six propositions is inconsistent with the original public meaning. Some people, who are not originalists or not only originalists, care about historical traditions and long-standing practices. They want to know what has been done since (say) 1850 or 1900 or 1950. Traditions may or may not support the six propositions.[25] If they do not, one or another of the propositions might be questioned or even rejected. These various possibilities raise fundamental questions about constitutional interpretation.

At times, I will be putting some pressure on every one of the six propositions. But for purposes of discussion, let us start with the (correct) assumption that they are generally or broadly right, and that they capture the separation of powers as the US Constitution understands it.

Understood in terms of these six propositions, the separation of powers has nothing to do with checks and balances.[26] It is genuinely about *separation as such.* So understood, it is not fully descriptive of the US Constitution, which mixes separation of powers with checks and balances.[27] It follows that, even if each of the six propositions remains a plausible reading of that Constitution, the constitutional text and current doctrine require important qualifications. For example, Congress exercises the judicial power insofar as the Senate conducts trials in the aftermath of impeachment in the House of Representatives. In addition, the executive branch does, in fact, exercise judicial power—a great deal of it. And in some respects, the judicial branch might be thought to exercise a bit of legislative power.[28] I will have a few things to say about these points.

I will be covering a great deal of ground in chapters 2, 3, and 4, and it will be useful to keep two general ideas in mind. First, each of the six propositions rests on eminently reasonable judgments about various institutions and their likely performance, capacities, and incentives. Above all, protection of liberty is an overriding goal, and protection of deliberative democracy is almost equally central. Second, those reasonable judgments are based on empirical projections, involving the capacities and likely performance of various institutions; though reasonable, the projections may not always be right. We can readily imagine one or another time and place in which one or another of the six propositions might be rejected.

I do not believe that the time is now or that the place is here. I do not even believe that the time is anywhen or that the place is anywhere—but still. Here as elsewhere, Schmitt's rejection of the separation of powers, and the experience of fascism under Hitler, offer the right warnings.

2 WHAT THE LEGISLATURE CANNOT DO

Suppose that Congress enacts a law making something a crime—say, disclosing classified information, or failing to file tax forms, or writing a book about the separation of powers. After that law is enacted, the decision whether to prosecute people for that crime is made by another branch of government, not by Congress itself. That is an important safeguard of liberty. The executive branch, with its own incentives and traditions, is required to make a separate decision about enforcement. It might decline to proceed at all.

THE LEGISLATURE MAY NOT EXERCISE THE EXECUTIVE POWER

The result is that citizens have the protection that comes from the need for concurrence from two layers of government, not just one. Prosecutorial discretion, prominently including the discretion not to act, is a crucial safeguard of freedom. As Attorney General (and later Justice) Robert Jackson put it: "With the law books filled with a great assortment of crimes, a prosecutor stands a fair chance of finding at least a technical violation of some act on the part of almost anyone."[1] One of Jackson's particular concerns was what he called "the most dangerous power of the prosecutor," which is

> that he will pick people that he thinks he should get, rather than pick cases that need to be prosecuted. With the law books filled with a great assortment of crimes, a prosecutor stands a fair chance of finding at least a technical violation of some act on the part of almost anyone. In such a case, it is not a question of discovering the commission of a crime and then looking for the man who has

committed it, it is a question of picking the man and then searching the law books, or putting investigators to work, to pin some offense on him. It is in this realm-in which the prosecutor picks some person whom he dislikes or desires to embarrass, or selects some group of unpopular persons and then looks for an offense, that the greatest danger of abuse of prosecuting power lies. It is here that law enforcement becomes personal, and the real crime becomes that of being unpopular with the predominant or governing group, being attached to the wrong political views, or being personally obnoxious to or in the way of the prosecutor himself.[2]

For liberty, that is bad news. For liberty, the good news is that a prosecutor, focused on offenses rather than offenders, can always say: "This is not worth my time." Or: "This is a place for mercy." Or: "I will go after the most serious offenses, not the most trivial." Imagine a system in which each and every crime was prosecuted, or in which the national legislature was put in a position to decide which crimes to prosecute, or in which particular people were targeted by prosecutors who sought to discover whether they committed any crime, ever. Liberty would be in grave danger.

Regulations issued by the executive branch may not be as dramatic as criminal statutes, but they can be analyzed similarly. Congress might authorize the Department of Health and Human Services to set forth regulations governing some sector of the economy—say, doctors and hospitals. For doctors and hospitals, that might be worrisome or scary. But the department has discretion to set priorities, and it might well have discretion not to issue those regulations at all.[3] The department might say, "not now." It might even say, "not ever." Here too, there is a potential safeguard of liberty. The regulatory enterprise might be an unjustified burden on the relevant sector; it might squelch freedom. And Congress itself might be aware of that. It might be counting on the second layer to ensure against excessive intrusiveness. The same can be said with respect to violations of regulations. The executive branch might say: "This one is just not worth the trouble."

A personal word: Under President Barack Obama, I served as the administrator of the White House Office of Information and Regulatory Affairs. That isn't a very exciting name, but the office oversees federal regulations from administrative agencies: the Department of Agriculture, the Department of Labor, the Department of Justice, the Department of State, the Environmental Protection Agency, the Department of Homeland Security, and many more. On numerous occasions, I told agencies "not now" or even "no"—not because of my personal views, necessarily, but because I knew that President Obama and his team did not want to impose regulations of that kind at that time. On occasion, I would walk around the White House and tell people, "It's economic growth time; it's not regulation time"— which was a signal, back in 2009 and 2010, that we were facing a recession and we would need to be careful about regulations. We wanted to give private liberty (of multiple kinds) room to flourish.

The argument against execution of the laws by the legislature is fundamentally right, and I mean to praise it, not to bury it. Note, however, that it conceals some contestable premises, and on certain assumptions, the two layers might be a cure that is worse than the disease. Fascists tend to think so. But they are not alone in thinking so.

Let us assume that the executive branch is lazy, corrupt, or otherwise ill-motivated. Let us assume that it does not want to enforce the law when the law really should be enforced, or that it has a bad or perverse agenda. Perhaps it is in thrall to well-organized private groups. Perhaps it does not much care about occupational safety and health. Perhaps it does not care about clean air. Perhaps it does not care about civil rights.

If so, we might well be better off if the legislature could exercise executive power. Whether two layers are a salutary protection of liberty or instead a form of overkill depends on judgments about how executive power is likely to be exercised. If the legislature would exercise executive power well, or if the executive is wrongheaded or arbitrary, then the two layers would be nothing to celebrate.

There are underlying disputes here about the right conception of *liberty*.[4] You might believe that liberty requires immunity from government intrusion ("private liberty"), or you might also or instead believe that liberty requires government help or protection. Suppose we agree that, though private liberty is exceedingly important, liberty is also compromised if people are subject to unsafe working conditions, dirty air, dirty water, and discrimination. Suppose we believe that the New Deal, with its emphasis on education, employment, and social security, had something like the right conception of liberty,[5] or at least had something to add. If so, we might fear that the executive branch's discretion, and its ability to say "not now" or "never," is a threat to liberty, properly conceived. That thought helps explain some of the shifts in the understandings of the separation of powers that occurred during the New Deal, with an increase in the discretionary policymaking authority of the executive branch and with the rise in the policymaking authority of independent regulatory commissions.[6]

Consider, in this light, continuing debates about whether courts can review executive inaction. Suppose that the executive just does not act. It does not protect against dirty air, dirty water, or unsafe working conditions. It sits on its hands. (Maybe the president directs an agency to do that.) On one view, agency inaction is in an altogether different category from agency action, because it does not involve the exercise of coercive authority over citizens.[7] That view is controversial, and rightly so. On a competing view, agency inaction is not different, in principle, from agency action; if an agency fails to act, it fails to protect people from harm (and threatens their liberty, properly conceived).

These are important debates. But let us not lose sight of the central point. The requirement of concurrence and action from the executive, before the menacing weight of government can be brought to bear, is a crucial safeguard of a crucial form of liberty.

THE LEGISLATURE MAY NOT EXERCISE THE JUDICIAL POWER

Legislatures are not courts, and they are not allowed to act like courts. But what does it mean to say that the legislature may not exercise the judicial power? What is "the judicial power"?

On one view, the answer is simple: The judicial power is the *power to adjudicate disputes*, and the legislature may not adjudicate disputes.[8] That is also a crucial safeguard of liberty. Suppose that members of Congress think that Olson has committed a crime, and they want Olson to go to jail. The separation of powers means that the legislature cannot engage in adjudication. Olson gets the benefit of a real court, with the traditional characteristics, practices, and norms of the judiciary, not a political body. Those traditions preserve a degree of independence and fairness. They protect Olson against the mob.

Or suppose that there is a dispute between Jones and Smith. If so, it too should be resolved by a real court. The same is true if there is a dispute between Jones and the Internal Revenue Service, or between Jones and the Environmental Protection Agency, or between Jones and the Department of Homeland Security. Members of Congress want to be reelected. If they rule for one or another side, they might lose votes. If Congress is resolving that dispute, the electoral connection might well distort the process of adjudica-tion. We cannot have faith in the fairness of that process if legislators are in charge of it.

The central point seems clear if judicial officers are independent—that is, if they are protected from political reprisal. Judicial independence is cen-tral to the separation of powers. But the central point holds even if judges are themselves elected. Judges always have their own traditions and con-straints, and those traditions and constraints are well-suited to the process of adjudication—real, rather than Potemkin.[9] Liberty depends on that.

ALEXANDER HAMILTON

On another view, the judicial power centrally involves the (authoritative) *interpretation of what the law is*,[10] and here things start to get a bit more com-plicated. Suppose that Congress enacts a law that may or may not be con-stitutional. If Congress is entitled to resolve the constitutional issue, then we cannot exactly expect an impartial judgment! Congress is most unlikely to think that (a) a statute for which it has voted is an excellent idea and (b) that very statute is unconstitutional. An independent tribunal, assessing the constitutional objection, seems far better.

Alexander Hamilton put it this way:

> If it be said that the legislative body are themselves the constitutional judges of their own powers and that the construction they put upon them is conclusive upon the other departments it may be answered that this cannot be the natural presumption where it is not to be collected from any particular provisions in the Constitution. It is not otherwise to be supposed that the Constitution could intend to enable the representatives of the people to substitute their *will* to that of their constituents. It is far more rational to suppose that the courts were designed to be an intermediate body between the people and the legislature in order, among other things, to keep the latter within the limits assigned to their authority.[11]

That's a famous passage, and it is terrific. Still, Hamilton does not quite spell out the logic here. Why, exactly, is that "more rational to suppose"? The answer must be that with respect to the meaning of the Constitution, courts are relatively impartial, and that "an intermediate body" is better situated to keep the legislature within the bounds of its authority. For reasons just sketched, that is an eminently plausible answer.[12] If the legislature is mak-ing a judgment about whether its own actions are constitutional, how objective can it be? It will undoubtedly be motivated to say that the answer to that question is an emphatic *yes*. (See chapter 11 for some details.)

Here as well, the various judgments are empirical speculations, not logical truths. Of course, it is true that Congress has an obligation to follow the Constitution, which means that it is supposed to assess the relevant legal issues, even if its assessment is not authoritative.[13] It has an independent obligation to interpret the law so as to ensure that it remains faithful to it, which means that it exercises some kind of judicial power, even if its exercise of that power is not binding or authoritative.[14] That is a solemn obligation.

Regrettably, I can report from my various times in Washington that members of Congress do not always take that obligation so seriously. Most of them are not trained in constitutional law. Many of them think: "Well, the courts will handle the constitutional issue." Many of them think: "It's a good idea, so surely it's constitutional." In fact, I have not seen a single case in which even one member of Congress thought, "I think it is a great idea, but it's unconstitutional, so I will vote against it." There must be some such cases, to be sure, but they are not common. All this attests to the sense of saying that the legislature may not exercise the judicial power.

Nonetheless, we could imagine institutional judgments that would cut hard the other way. Suppose, for example, that legislatures did in fact take their constitutional responsibilities exceedingly seriously and would be most unlikely to act in ways that violated the founding document. Suppose too that courts had agendas of their own and that they would interpret the Constitution in a way that reflected their own judgments of policy and principle. Under such assumptions, a prohibition on the exercise of judicial authority by legislatures would produce less, rather than more, in the way of fidelity to the Constitution. That's fair enough, and it is especially fair to complain that judicial interpretations of the Constitution may be affected by judicial judgments of policy and principle. Still, we might reasonably think that because of the likely motivations of the two institutions, it is best to give judges, and not legislators, the ultimate authority to pronounce on the meaning of the Constitution.

INTERPRETATION

There is another complication, and here again we are going to have to get a bit technical. To assess Hamilton's argument, we need a theory of constitutional interpretation. His argument might seem to work best if we are public meaning originalists. In ascertaining the original public meaning, we might suppose that courts are likely to be more impartial than legislatures, though, for the reasons just stated, that is not inevitable.

But imagine that judges embrace a different theory. Suppose that they are moral readers (as some people think that they should be),[15] seeking to give the founding document the best imaginable moral reading. Moral readers would think that the First Amendment, protecting the freedom of speech, should be given a moral reading, one that is not bound to history but that changes over time, perhaps expanding that form of freedom (to include, perhaps, even dangerous speech, or sexually explicit speech). If we are moral readers, the case for forbidding legislators to exercise judicial power might seem to be greatly strengthened—or greatly weakened. Things get complicated here, and in a hurry. Suppose we think that moral readings by unelected judges are illegitimate[16] and that legislators will follow the original public meaning and are competent public meaning originalists. If so, we might well want legislators to exercise judicial authority. And if *both* legislators and courts are moral readers, the question is which will produce the better moral readings. There is no abstract answer to that question.[17] Political accountability might be a virtue; it might be a vice.

Or suppose that judges believe in representation-reinforcing judicial review, which means that they seek to improve the operations of the democratic process.[18] In seeking to do that, perhaps they protect the right to vote; perhaps they protect the right to free speech. Suppose that they are very good indeed at that sort of thing, and suppose we think that representation-reinforcing judicial review is an excellent idea. If so, we might want to forbid legislators from exercising judicial power, at least in the sense that we will want to insist that they do not get the final say on the meaning of constitutional provisions. But there are two big *ifs* there.

BEYOND CONSTITUTIONAL INTERPRETATION

Let us bracket the complexities here and assume (as we should) that Hamilton is broadly right. If so, the principle does not apply only to judicial review for constitutionality. Who interprets laws enacted by Congress? Who gets the final word on what those laws mean? If we are committed to the rule of law,[19] we will be quite wary of a situation in which those who enact the law are also charged with its interpretation. How can they possibly be objective?

To be sure, the legislature may be in a privileged position with respect to intended meaning. It might know what its intentions are. But if the question is *what a statute means to ordinary readers*,[20] then courts might well be in a better position than legislatures are. And from the standpoint of the rule of law, that is indeed the question.

Focused on the natural or ordinary meaning of texts, judges should be in a far superior position to those who voted for legislation. Of course, there is no inevitable conclusion here on who is likely to perform best. To return to one of our themes: We could easily imagine a judiciary that would be highly reliable; we could easily imagine a judiciary, armed with its own convictions and willing to deploy them, that would not be reliable at all. Still, it is reasonable to think, once more, that judges, with their customs and traditions, are in a far better position to make a fair judgment than legislators, who are concerned with reelection and politics.

CANONS AND CANNONS

Apart from judicial review for constitutionality, courts might use "canons of interpretation" that have deep roots in traditions or constitutional principles, but that legislatures might not endorse or apply in particular cases. These canons can be important. Consider here the following:

- The rule of lenity, which says that criminal statutes will be interpreted favorably to those accused of crimes (not because we like them, but to ensure that they get fair notice)
- The Avoidance Canon, which says that laws will be interpreted so as to avoid serious constitutional doubts[21]
- The canon against retroactivity, which says that laws will not be understood to apply to conduct that was lawful when it occurred[22]
- The canon against extraterritorial application of national law, which says that domestic law will not apply outside of the territorial boundaries of the United States[23]

Judges might (and do) wield these canons, very much for the better; legislators might be indifferent or hostile to them.

Here is Hamilton again, and what he says is full of implications for the separation of powers:

> But it is not with a view to infractions of the Constitution only that the independence of the judges may be an essential safeguard against the effects of occasional

ill humors in the society. These sometimes extend no farther than to the injury of the private rights of particular classes of citizens, by unjust and partial laws. Here also the firmness of the judicial magistracy is of vast importance in mitigating the severity and confining the operation of such laws. It not only serves to moderate the immediate mischiefs of those which may have been passed but it operates as a check upon the legislative body in passing them; who, perceiving that obstacles to the success of iniquitous intention are to be expected from the scruples of the courts, are in a manner compelled, by the very motives of the injustice they meditate, to qualify their attempts.[24]

This is a striking passage insofar as it emphasizes the role of the judiciary in guarding "against the effects of occasional ill humors" and in "mitigating the severity and confining the operation of" law. It is endlessly instructive to compare Hamilton to Schmitt; let us stand with Hamilton. Here again, liberty is a defining value. On plausible (if optimistic) assumptions about how courts work, it is entirely right to endorse the idea that legislators cannot exercise judicial authority, because they would act in a way that would undermine the rule of law, properly understood. Of course, it is true that some of the concerns raised about judicial review of statutes for constitutionality apply here as well.

Still, let us cry it from the rooftops: The judicial authority is for judges, not legislators, and legislators cannot exercise that authority.

3 WHAT THE EXECUTIVE CANNOT DO

Now let us turn to the executive. What is it forbidden to do? In many ways, that is the largest question of all, because the executive branch is the most dangerous branch (see chapter 6). Because it is run by a single person, it is in a unique position to do all kinds of horrifying things. Would-be tyrants, take note; would-be defenders of liberty, please unite.

THE EXECUTIVE MAY NOT EXERCISE THE JUDICIAL POWER

The initial question, once more, is the meaning of the term *the judicial power*. Let us begin by assuming that the term refers to authoritative interpretation of the meaning of federal law. In this context, we confront Schmitt directly: "The real Führer is always a judge. Out of Führerdom flows judgeship." My gosh. Not so. Not at all. In a system of separation of powers, both of these statements are anathema.

Suppose that a law makes something a crime. Now suppose that the question is whether someone—say, you—has actually committed that crime. If the executive charges you with a crime, then an independent court is available to answer whether you have, in fact, committed a crime. That is a crucial safeguard of liberty. If the executive, who is charging you, can decide whether you violated the law, then freedom is at grave risk. The fact that the executive may not exercise the judicial power is an essential safeguard of liberty, as people all over the world learn every decade.

Now suppose that the Environmental Protection Agency (EPA) is issuing some regulation under the Clean Air Act (CAA). The regulation might involve particulate matter, ozone, or greenhouse gases. In a standard case, the regulation might be challenged on the ground that it is inconsistent with the law and is also "arbitrary and capricious." If the executive could resolve those questions and thus exercise judicial power, then the rule of law would be in jeopardy. The executive has every incentive to resolve difficult issues (and perhaps not-so-difficult issues) in its own favor. Once more, liberty itself might well be at risk.

CAREFUL

We do have to be careful here. It is true that a well-functioning executive branch will be keenly alert to its obligations under the Constitution's Take Care Clause, and it will investigate the legal issues with care and conscientiousness. We could imagine a continuum of possibilities here, from an executive that is highly scrupulous with respect to the legal issues to one that is careless or excruciatingly self-serving. When I worked in the Department of Homeland Security from 2021 to 2024, I found that people were highly scrupulous. They did not want to violate the law. They were exceedingly careful. But in the annals of history, it is not difficult to find self-serving executive branch officials and malevolent executive branch officials, relatively indifferent to law.

There is another point. Suppose that the question is the meaning of a legal term like *diagnosis* or *source* or *calendar*. One view or another is not necessarily, or perhaps in any sense, in the executive's favor. It is often implausible to say that one or another view is self-serving. We have to be careful in saying that the executive, if it is biased, will choose an interpretation that serves its self-interest. Sometimes no interpretation will promote its self-interest.

Still, it is true that an executive branch that exercises judicial power is often acting as judge in its own cause, at least insofar as it is deciding on the legality of its own initiatives and practices. That is an excellent reason to separate execution of the law from interpretation of the law.

Similar things might be said about constitutional issues. We should hope that the executive branch will give careful consideration to the question of whether its regulations, or its actions more broadly, violate the founding document. But hope is one thing; reality is another. You can easily think of American presidents who did not care a whole lot about the Constitution. To be sure, caring about the Constitution is one of the jobs of the Attorney General and the Office of Legal Counsel within the Department of Justice—and general counsels within agencies, and those who work for them, explore constitutional questions essentially every day. But there is an inevitable risk that its judgments will ultimately be self-serving, and the president himself might override his lawyers. As they say, foxes should not guard henhouses—a point about both liberty and the rule of law.

Under Presidents Jimmy Carter and Ronald Reagan, I worked as a (young!) lawyer in the Office of Legal Counsel. I tried my best, as did everyone with whom I worked. But at the time, and in the decades since, the Office of Legal Counsel has not (let us say) always been impartial in its judgments about the meaning of federal law. Its interpretations have tended to favor the president and his views. It hasn't been Nazi Germany, not at all, not nearly—but still, an independent court is essential. (The year 2025 provided a large number of examples.)

The analysis must be different if the executive is seeking to decide whether acts of Congress are inconsistent with the Constitution. We might think that in such circumstances, the risk of bias is reduced, because the executive is not assessing itself. But again, the executive has its own goals, and it lacks the traditions and constraints of courts. People who work for the president are not protected by tenure and salary guarantees. It is reasonable to think that their constitutional judgments will be badly skewed—and imperfectly reliable. The same could be true for courts, of course, and there are no logical proofs here. But if we are to choose which institution will exercise the judicial power, it makes a lot of sense to say, with Hamilton: *courts*.

DON'T THINK OF AN ELEPHANT

It is also true, and fundamental, that the executive power and the judicial power are separated, in the sense that the executive initiates cases (including prosecutions), and the judges decide on both facts and law. If the Department of Justice thinks that you have committed a crime, it cannot put you in jail just because it wants to do that. It has to prove its case before an independent tribunal (often with a jury).

That was a short paragraph, but it is one of the most important in this book. Here again, the separation of powers safeguards liberty. People have an opportunity to defend themselves not before those who are charging them, but before a separate institution.

Still, there is a small elephant in the room. It will be noticed that every day, the executive does exercise judicial power, *in the sense that it engages in adjudication.* Consider, for example, the Social Security Administration and the National Labor Relation Board. This area of law is unusually complex, and there do not appear to be clear rules. But after the Supreme Court's decision in *Crowell v. Benson*,[1] it is clear that at least some adjudicatory action by executive agencies does not offend Article III. Does this mean that the executive may, in fact, exercise judicial authority?

The short answer is *yes*. The longer and better answer is that the executive may exercise judicial authority, more or less, but *only (and this is crucial) if it is sufficiently constrained and supervised by Article III courts.*[2] The relevant set of constraints and supervisions is meant to protect liberty. The many twists and turns, and the instability of current law, need not detain us here. (They will detain us a bit more in chapter 8.) Some people are skeptical of *Crowell v. Benson* and think that it gravely undermines the separation of powers. Other people think that the decision, and the exercise of some adjudicatory power by executive agencies, is consistent with long-standing separation-of-powers traditions and maintains fidelity with Article III *so long as Article III judges are available to require fidelity to law and also to ensure that agency fact-finding has a sufficient basis in law.*

For what it is worth, I tend to agree with the latter view. For present purposes, the key point is that, however heated, these are ultimately disputes among most-of-the-time friends, both committed to maintaining separation between executive and adjudicatory authority.

Let's turn away from the trees and look at the forest. By virtue of its distinctive role, the executive is not likely to be the most reliable interpreter of the law. (That is putting it mildly.) Because they are judges, judges are likely to be a lot better. Of course, there are no guarantees here, but Schmitt's view offers a cautionary note, one that strongly supports the view that the executive may not exercise the judicial power. *Unhinging the state*, to adopt Schmitt's phrase, is a terrific idea.

THE EXECUTIVE MAY NOT EXERCISE THE LEGISLATIVE POWER

Now we turn to what seems to me to be the most important restriction of all. Congress has "all legislative powers." The executive branch does not. But what are *all legislative powers*? What is *legislative power*?

Let us start very simply, by understanding the term to refer to lawmaking as Article I sees and specifies it. The executive cannot "make law." To be sure, it can issue binding rules, at least under current law—but if and only if Congress authorizes it to do so. When we say that the executive cannot exercise the legislative power, then, what are we forbidding?

Here is the central answer. To act, the executive generally needs a permission slip, in the form of authorizing legislation. Congress must say: "You can do that." So the court ruled in 1952 in *Youngstown Sheet & Steel Tube Co.*,[3] which is probably the most important separation-of-powers decision in US history. It follows that the executive cannot address crime, air pollution, inflation, climate change, immigration, or highway safety on its own. The basic idea here is that the national legislature, with its distinctive form of accountability, must authorize the executive branch to act. We can (and should) associate that idea with the goal of ensuring a deliberative democracy, specified in the composition of the House and Senate, the requirement of bicameralism, and the opportunity for presidential signature or veto.

The requirement of legislative authorization should also be seen as a check on *group polarization*, the process by which like-minded people, engaged in discussion with one another, sometimes go to extremes.[4] People in the executive branch might get all charged up, thinking that an initiative or a reform is a terrific idea (in, say, the area of immigration or environmental protection)—but they cannot act unless the legislature tells them that they can.

The prohibition on exercise of legislative authority by the executive branch should also be associated with the protection of liberty. Because it needs legislative permission, the executive cannot go after citizens, or their liberty, on its own. Insofar as we are seeking to understand the ban on the exercise of legislative power by the executive branch, that might be the most important justification of all. If we had to choose just one separation-of-powers principle as the first among equals, this one is the best candidate.

Even so, there is a counterargument. Suppose that national problems are serious and numerous. Suppose that by virtue of its composition and processes, the national legislature is simply unable to handle those problems.[5] The problem might be gridlock. The problem might be sheer complexity. In that light, we could imagine situations in which some people think that the exercise of legislative power by the executive branch is absolutely essential. If the executive branch is unable to exercise legislative power, serious and perhaps catastrophic problems will go unsolved.

This might be, and I think should be, dismissed as an unacceptably Schmittian point. But under American law, it is a fair cautionary note, and it has implications for several sets of current controversies. The first involves the nondelegation doctrine.[6] What kinds of constraints does Article I, section 1 impose on a grant of discretionary authority to the executive branch? If the executive branch is exercising broad discretion, is it exercising legislative authority? Some people think so; in their view, very broad discretionary authority simply *is* legislative authority.[7] Other people think not; in their view, even very broad discretionary authority counts as executive authority *if it is exercised under and pursuant to a legislative grant of discretion.*[8]

There is an intense debate about the historical pedigree, or not, of the nondelegation doctrine, understood as a restriction on the grant of discretionary authority to the executive, and I will have a lot to say about that in this book.[9] In brief: It now appears that historical support for that doctrine, so understood, is quite weak.[10] There is an equally intense debate about whether and to what extent aggressive judicial enforcement of the nondelegation doctrine would well serve the American people.[11] On one view, such enforcement would protect, at once, liberty and deliberative democracy (or self-government).[12] On another view, such enforcement would disable Congress from acting in such a way as to allow real problems to be solved.[13]

In my view, aggressive enforcement of the nondelegation doctrine would be a terrible, awful, stinky idea.[14] But one might accept that view while also insisting that the executive may not exercise legislative power, *in the sense that it may not make law* (and perhaps also in the sense that the most open-ended exercises of discretion are a violation of Article I, section 1).

There is also an intense debate about whether the executive has "emergency power."[15] In the area of foreign affairs, it is generally agreed that the president may act unilaterally to repel a sudden attack.[16] Suppose, however, that there is some kind of domestic crisis, involving (say) a pandemic, an internal rebellion, or potentially catastrophic environmental harm. May the president act on his own?[17] The general view is that he may not, but the door is not quite shut. There are unresolved questions of history and principle here.[18]

I say, keep that door shut! If there really is an emergency, the legislature is likely to authorize the president to respond. Deliberative democracy should be respected. If the president is allowed to act without legislative authorization, liberty is at excessive risk.

4 WHAT THE COURTS CANNOT DO

What are judges permitted to do? What are judges forbidden to do? We have seen some answers to the first question. Now let's focus on the second.

THE JUDICIARY MAY NOT EXERCISE THE LEGISLATIVE POWER

This principle might be the most intuitive of all. Courts are not legislatures, and they are not entitled to legislate. They cannot "make law." One reason for this principle is that judges lack the right kind of accountability. They are not elected. Consider the kinds of judgments that are involved in questions about (say) clean water, clean air, road safety, and immigration. Those judgments require democratic accountability, which judges lack. A system of deliberative democracy cannot tolerate lawmaking by judges.

Another reason, and an important one, is that judges do not have the requisite information: Lawmaking calls for acquisition of a lot of knowledge, and the adversarial process, well-suited to the resolution of disputes, is not well-suited to the development of legislation.[1] Call this the *epistemic argument* for the ban on the exercise of legislative authority by judges. In chapter 6, we will explore this argument in more detail.

Still, there are complications. Judges have long had common law authority. In property law, tort law, and contract law, judges make law incrementally and case-by-case. Even in the aftermath of the Supreme Court's decision in the *Erie* case, which denied that authority to federal courts,[2] something like the common law tradition is alive and well in American law.[3] Is the common law a form of legislation? Not technically and not formally in the sense of Article I, section 1—but it does involve what might well be described as the making of law. We can have learned discussions of the similarity between legislation, as such, and lawmaking through the common law—but still, the differences are real. In creating common law, courts may not always act incrementally, but they cannot produce a Clean Air Act, an Affordable Care Act, or an Inflation Reduction Act. The fact that they cannot exercise the legislative power is exceedingly important. They are not elected, and they do not know what they would need to know.

THE JUDICIARY MAY NOT EXERCISE THE EXECUTIVE POWER

In general, judges may not bring enforcement proceedings; in general, they may not make regulations. As in the case of the immediately preceding principle, one reason is, of course, accountability. The executive is subject to "We the People," which is an important safeguard. Another is (again) epistemic, particularly in the context of regulations. Development and issuance of regulations involving (say) carcinogens calls for a great deal of knowledge, which judges lack.

We could introduce some qualifications, but they do not undermine the basic claims, so let's not.

ON TYRANNY

Let's step back. Was Madison right? Is the accumulation of all powers—legislative, executive, and judicial—in the same hands rightly described as the very definition of tyranny? The arc of human history so suggests. We should unhinge the state, with the aid of the judiciary. We should do that in the name of liberty. We should also do that in the name of deliberative democracy.

The six separation-of-powers principles are critically important, but as the American constitutional order lives and breathes them, they have different degrees of firmness. We can raise a series of empirical and conceptual challenges to each of the principles. For example, the executive branch exercises broad discretion, and it creates binding rules. Still, it cannot produce actual legislation. The legislature may not exercise judicial power, and courts may not prosecute anyone. But the executive branch does adjudicate (a lot; take a look at the Social Security Administration), and in that sense it exercises judicial power. It would be possible and instructive to explore, in great detail, the precise content of each of the six principles and how they might be qualified.

I have attempted to sketch the underlying justifications for each of the six principles. All of them have a great deal to do with liberty. If the legislature cannot exercise executive authority, then citizens have two levels of protection, not one. (And the courts make for three.) If the executive cannot exercise legislative authority, then citizens are protected against a kind of absolutism. Even if Congress is allowed to grant the executive broad discretionary authority, it much matters that discretionary authority *must always be granted, not asserted*. If the executive cannot exercise judicial authority in the sense of issuing binding interpretations of the Constitution, federal statutes, and federal regulations, then we can secure important features of the rule of law. All the separation-of-powers principles also have a great deal to do with self-government and, in particular, with the idea of deliberative democracy.

At the same time, I have identified some complications. If legislators were perfectly reliable in their understanding of the meaning of legal texts, and if judges were likely to go off on larks of their own, then we might be a lot more enthusiastic about legislative exercise of judicial authority. If the legislature were blocked and unable to address serious social problems, then we might be prepared to welcome a little, or perhaps a lot, in the way of executive exercise of legislative authority. Institutional judgments are not a matter of logic or arithmetic.

In some times and places, one or more of the six propositions discussed here might be rejected.[4] But suppose that we care, as we should, about liberty and deliberative democracy. In most times and places, each and every one of the six propositions should be enthusiastically embraced.

5 THE PRESIDENT'S IMMUNITY

Suppose that the president of the United States commits a crime. For example, he might order his subordinates to kill his opponents, or perhaps to lock them up. You might think that because of the separation of powers, he can be held to account. You might think that no one is above the law. If so, you would be wrong.

How on earth did we get there? I aim to answer that question, and to do so in a way that is as charitable as possible to where we are—but we are not where we should be, not close.

In *Trump v. United States*,[1] the Supreme Court established a new separation-of-powers framework for assessing the question of whether the president is immune from the reach of criminal law. A key part of that framework involves a momentous shift. Before *Trump*, the immunity issue was analyzed by reference to the following question: Would subjecting the president to a legal proceeding compromise his ability to perform his constitutional functions?[2] For example, a criminal prosecution of a sitting president might be out-of-bounds for that reason. How can he serve as commander in chief if he is facing a jail sentence? The underlying theory might be that if the president faces a criminal prosecution, his ability to do his job would be seriously compromised. From the standpoint of the separation of powers, that is a good theory. That is the right question to ask.

After *Trump*, the immunity issue is analyzed, in significant part,[3] by reference to an altogether different question: Does some provision of the Constitution give the president unquestionable power, such that neither Congress nor courts may intrude on it? The new question is asked and resolved, in turn, with close reference to Justice Robert Jackson's famous concurring opinion in *Youngstown Sheet & Steel Tube Co. v. Sawyer*,[4] and in particular by reference to Justice Jackson's reference to rare situations in which the president has authority that is "conclusive" and "preclusive,"[5] such that no one may question it.

Youngstown was not, of course, about immunity at all. The question there was whether the president could seize the nation's steel mills, and divert them to military use, without clear congressional authorization. The Supreme Court ruled that he could not. In concurrence, Justice Jackson distinguished among three kinds of cases. The first is Category 1: When the president has congressional authorization, his authority is at its highest. The second is Category 2: When Congress has been silent, the president is in a kind of twilight zone, in which we need to know a lot of details. The third is Category 3: When the president is acting against congressional instructions, the president's authority is at its lowest. He needs "conclusive and preclusive" authority, which is rare indeed. Justice Jackson used those words not to recognize broad presidential power, but to suggest that the president would need to show that the Constitution gave him authority to act on its own. Justice Jackson was certainly not speaking about immunity.

A key moving part in *Trump*, and its most innovative feature, is its emphasis on Category 3: cases in which the president can act against the will of Congress if and when he has clear authority to do so under the Constitution. In *Trump*, the court linked that idea with the immunity issue.[6] Indeed, the court engaged in a form of constitutional alchemy, transforming several of its previous decisions (at least three[7]) into immunity rulings.

The result is a distortion, not a rendering, of the idea of separation of powers. In a way, the court took us back to Carl Schmitt. That's tough talk, I know, but it's true.

FAST AND FURIOUS

The core of the court's *Trump* analysis is given in a stunningly brief section early in its opinion. The court began by listing the president's constitutionally specified duties, which include commanding the armed forces and granting reprieves and pardons. That's fair enough. After offering that list, the court, quoting Justice Jackson, stated that when the president's authority is granted by the Constitution, it is sometimes "conclusive and preclusive."[8] If so, neither Congress nor the courts can control the president's authority and discretion: "Once it is determined that the President acted within the scope of his exclusive authority, his discretion in exercising such authority cannot be subject to further judicial examination."[9] This is essentially a claim about unreviewability: *No one can review the president's decision.*

We should return here to the origins of that large idea of "conclusive and preclusive" authority. Here is what Justice Jackson actually said: "When the President takes measures incompatible with the expressed or implied will of Congress, his power is at its lowest ebb, for then he can rely only upon his own constitutional powers minus any constitutional powers of Congress over the matter. Courts can sustain exclusive presidential control in such a case only by disabling the Congress from acting upon the subject. Presidential claim to a power at once so conclusive and preclusive must be scrutinized with caution, for what is at stake is the equilibrium established by our constitutional system."[10]

That's a mouthful. The basic idea is that sometimes the president does something that is inconsistent with the will of Congress, and when he does, he will usually lose. His only hope is to say that the Constitution gives him power to act on his own. That explains Justice Jackson's insistence that when the president acts inconsistently with Congress's will, his power is "at its lowest ebb." He adds that presidential claims to "conclusive and preclusive" power must be scrutinized carefully, because something fundamental is at stake: "the equilibrium established by our constitutional system." Justice Jackson did not want to disturb that equilibrium. In *Trump*, by contrast, the court was far more hospitable to a claim of "conclusive and preclusive" power. Indeed, it seemed to do a few somersaults, or at least a high jump (the Fosbury flop?), to accept that claim.

As its first example of what it had in mind, the court returned to the president's pardon power.[11] It noted that during and after the Civil War, President Lincoln offered a full pardon, including restoration of property rights, to those who engaged in the rebellion if they swore an oath of allegiance to the union.[12] Congress later enacted a law that made it unlawful to use the president's pardon as evidence of the restoration of property rights.[13] In *United States v. Klein*,[14] the court invalidated that law on separation-of-powers grounds.[15] It said that the law infringed on the power of the president, to whom "alone is entrusted the power of a pardon."[16] In *Klein*, the court reasoned that if the president can grant pardons, he can also decide what those pardons entail.[17] If he decides that a pardon includes restoration of property rights, Congress cannot overturn that decision or take steps to reduce its effect. "Now it is clear that the legislature cannot change the effect of such a pardon any more than the executive can change a law."[18]

In the view of the *Trump* court, *Klein* was essentially an immunity ruling. *Klein* saw the president's exercise of the pardon power as immune from scrutiny from another branch. This was a striking and innovative use of *Klein*, which (like *Youngstown*) is not naturally seen as an immunity case at all.

We should immediately note that *Klein* was an exceedingly narrow holding. If a president decides that the beneficiary of a pardon (say, Hunter Biden) is not only free from (say) a jail sentence but must also have his property rights restored, then we might say that Congress cannot interfere with that decision without also saying much about the boundaries of the pardon power. The *Trump* court read *Klein* quite broadly, and in a way that strikes a hard blow against the separation of powers. I will turn to this issue in short order.

In *Trump*, the court added that the pardon power is analogous to the removal power, with which Congress also cannot interfere.[19] We know, for example, that Congress cannot restrict the president's authority to remove various high-level executive officials, such as the secretary of state, the secretary of defense, and the attorney general.[20] They work for him. Congress could not say that such officials can be discharged only for good cause, and it certainly could not make it a crime for the president to discharge such officials without good cause. "Congress cannot act on, and courts cannot examine, the President's actions within his 'conclusive and preclusive' constitutional authority."[21] Thus, Congress lacks power to "criminalize the President's actions within his exclusive presidential power," which means that he "is absolutely immune from criminal prosecution for conduct within his exclusive sphere of constitutional authority."[22] (Note well: This does not quite follow. What would follow is that Congress lacks power to regulate that conduct, which means that as applied to the president, the statute is invalid.)

Let us note the distinctive argument here. The removal cases are certainly about Article II authority, but (to return to one of my themes) they are not naturally taken as immunity cases at all. It is highly innovative, even ingenious, to take them that way. Consistent with previous immunity cases,[23] it would be possible to say that a *sitting* president has immunity from a criminal prosecution. The reason is not because he is acting within an authority that is "conclusive and preclusive," but because an ongoing criminal prosecution would make it impossible or very difficult for him to exercise his constitutional functions. How can someone do the job of president if he has to defend himself, in court, against a criminal prosecution? Maybe he just cannot. This has in fact been the long-standing position of the Department of Justice.[24]

Even if we accept that position, we have not resolved the question whether a *former* president is immune from a criminal prosecution. It may not be entirely wild to argue that he is, on the ground that mere anticipation of a possible criminal prosecution, at some point in the future, would make it difficult or impossible for the president to exercise his constitutional functions. But that seems like a big stretch; it would be more natural to conclude the opposite.

The court's separation-of-powers analysis here, emphasizing presidential powers that are "conclusive and preclusive," is fast and furious. Let's slow down a bit.

CRIMES

Imagine that Congress makes it a crime for the president to pardon anyone convicted of crimes in connection with the events of January 6, 2021. Imagine that the law, though prospective only, extends to all presidents in office. Would such a law amount to an impermissible intrusion on the president's authority? Would it violate the separation of powers?

The text of the Constitution does not answer these questions. It says that the president "shall have Power to grant Reprieves and Pardons for Offences against the United States, except in Cases of Impeachment." By itself, that grant of "Power" does not tell us much about what, if anything, Congress can do in the relevant domain. To be sure, Congress could not *deny* the pardon power to the president; it seems safe to insist that Congress could not say that in a certain period, no pardons may be given. But could Congress say that certain kinds of crimes could not be pardoned? As a matter of semantics, the text of the Constitution is not entirely clear on that question.

It would be possible to imagine a grant of the pardon power to the president, in the constitutional text, accompanied by a clear (background) understanding that the national legislature *is entitled to define the kinds of crimes that are subject to that power.* Maybe Congress could forbid pardons for treason, for actual or attempted assassination of high-level officials, or for other crimes that strike at the heart of national security or the democratic order. (There is an argument that it could.) Or perhaps Congress could make it a crime for the president to solicit or to accept a bribe in return for a pardon. ("If you give me $5 million, I will give you a pardon!") I think Congress could do that. If it did, the pardon would be effective—but the president would be subject to criminal punishment. In *Trump*, the court was reckless to have resolved this issue with a kind of ipse dixit and without anything resembling analysis.

How should the issue have been resolved? In *Trump*, the court should not have resolved it, because it was not presented. If we are originalists, we would look, of course, at the original public meaning of the pardon power. We would ask: According to the original public meaning, did Congress have the authority to limit the kinds of crimes for which pardons would be acceptable? For originalists, that question would require historical investigation.

Now suppose that Congress can, in fact, restrict the pardon power in certain ways and does, in fact, make it a crime for the president to accept a bribe in return for a pardon. Might a criminal prosecution be brought against a sitting president for violating that statute? We could easily imagine a holding that while in office, the president may not be subjected to prosecution. As noted, this has been the long-standing position of the Department of Justice. But a former president would be another matter. To be sure, it could be argued that the very prospect of a criminal indictment would impose an intolerable chill on the president in discharging his duties, so that the ex ante effect of the statute would be a violation of Article II. But so long as the restriction is sufficiently narrow, that would be a challenging argument to make.

HORROR

Now let us broaden the viewscreen. Suppose that the president directs the attorney general to investigate his political opponents and to prosecute them for wrongdoing. Suppose that it is unmistakably clear that the political opponents have not committed a crime and that the president is acting only for one reason: to exact retribution. Suppose finally that Congress has made it a crime for the president to engage in this behavior and has defined the crime with sufficient specificity. It seems clear that on the *Trump* court's analysis, Congress cannot constitutionally do that. But that seems wild. Why did the court rule as it did?

In *Trump*, the court observed that President Trump "allegedly attempted to leverage the Justice Department's power and authority to convince certain States to replace their legitimate electors with Trump's fraudulent slates of electors."[25] To carry out that plan, it was alleged that "Trump met with the Acting Attorney General and other senior Justice Department and White House officials to discuss investigating purported election fraud and sending a letter from the Department to those States regarding such fraud." We could easily imagine a ruling that a *sitting* president could not be subjected to a criminal proceeding for engaging in that conduct. I think that such a ruling would be right. But the *Trump* court went much further. It said that a *former* president enjoys immunity for engaging in that conduct.

In the court's view, those allegations "plainly implicate Trump's 'conclusive and preclusive' authority." (Really?) The same, the court said, is true of President Trump's threat to remove the acting attorney general. (Really?) As the court saw things, the president's engagement with the Department of Justice, on questions involving investigation and prosecution, is part of the core of presidential authority (that is a fair point); the legislature may not question it at all, nor may the courts (that is not at all obvious).

We should be able to agree that under existing law, the president has unrestricted power to remove the attorney general (see chapter 8); we might even be able to agree that under Article II, Congress cannot limit that power in any way. But it emphatically does not follow that Congress cannot subject a former president to criminal punishment for certain kinds of demands on or interactions with the attorney general. If a president asks the attorney general to proceed against political opponents, or asks the secretary of defense to use the armed services to kill journalists, what grounds the idea that the president's authority is "conclusive and preclusive"? The court pointed to nothing at all—not text, not the original understanding, not historical practice, not considerations of constitutional structure. The text is indeterminate. The court did not investigate either the original understanding or historical practice. Considerations of constitutional structure, and of separation of powers, could plausibly be taken to point either way. In fact, they point more plausibly against immunity in such horrific cases.

If we are following Justice Jackson, and his evident caution about Category 3, then the president would not have unilateral authority here, against the will of Congress, unless the Constitution speaks plainly. The court offered no reason to think that the Constitution does that. The distance from Justice Jackson could not be greater.

MOTIVATING ERROR

What, then, motivated the court's terrible conclusion? Any answer is speculative, but a remarkable passage, late in the opinion, seems to offer a clue. The passage occurs in the context of a response to the argument, found in the dissents, that the court's broad immunity ruling would authorize and legitimate presidential wrongdoing:

> The dissents overlook the more likely prospect of an Executive Branch that cannibalizes itself, with each successive President free to prosecute his predecessors, yet unable to boldly and fearlessly carry out his duties for fear that he may be next. For instance, Section 371—which has been charged in this case—is a broadly worded criminal statute that can cover "any conspiracy for the purpose of impairing, obstructing or defeating the lawful function of any department of Government." Virtually every President is criticized for insufficiently enforcing some aspect of federal law (such as drug, gun, immigration, or environmental laws). An enterprising prosecutor in a new administration may assert that a previous President violated that broad statute. Without immunity, such types of prosecutions of ex-Presidents could quickly become routine. The enfeebling of the Presidency and our Government that would result from such a cycle of factional strife is exactly what the Framers intended to avoid. Ignoring those risks, the dissents are instead content to leave the preservation of our system of separated powers up to the good faith of prosecutors.[26]

The key concern here is "an Executive Branch that cannibalizes itself, with each successive President free to prosecute his predecessors, yet unable to boldly and fearlessly carry out his duties for fear that he may be next." By itself, that idea seems fair and important—but unmoored from the Constitution itself. The court tried to forge a link by indicating that the "enfeebling of the Presidency and our Government that would result from such a cycle of factional strife is exactly what the Framers intended to avoid." But that is a big stretch. It is true, of course, that the framers intended to avoid enfeebling of the presidency and the national government. It is also true that they were focused on the problem of factional strife.[27] But those concerns operate at far too high a level of generality to support the particular conclusions and concerns in *Trump*.

Those concerns, I suggest, represent an identifiable strand in US constitutional law, a strand that unifies a number of separation-of-powers decisions in recent years.[28] The underlying problem is one of *democratic disorder*, and the Supreme Court might be thought to have a distinctive role in quieting it. In a way, that role is a close cousin of the representation-reinforcing role for the judiciary that John Hart Ely famously developed in *Democracy and Distrust*.[29] Ely saw the court's role as responding to democratic deficits, in the form of interference with political rights and exclusions of identifiable groups or diminutions of their political power.[30] For those who are concerned with democratic disorder, the motivating idea is quite different. It is that democratic processes are occasionally prone to instability, even dangerous instability, and it is a legitimate role of the Supreme Court to produce more in the way of order. The idea that democracies are prone to disorder is, of course, an old idea, not a new one.[31] What is new is the notion that part of the role of the Supreme Court is to counteract or reduce it.

Bush v. Gore[32] is probably the most famous example of a Supreme Court decision that is best understood as a response to pending disorder. It arrived amid a chaotic situation, in which the nation was torn about how to resolve the contested presidential election between George W. Bush and Al Gore. The court declared a halt to the recount in Florida, even though it was unable to point to a solid constitutional source for its ruling. In retrospect, it seems clear that the court was seeking to stabilize an unstable situation.

Trump v. Anderson,[33] ruling that Colorado could not deny ballot access to Trump, belongs in the same category. Here is the key passage; what is noteworthy is its pragmatism—that is, its focus on consequences:

> Conflicting state outcomes concerning the same candidate could result not just from differing views of the merits, but from variations in state law governing the proceedings that are necessary to make Section 3 disqualification determinations. Some States might allow a Section 3 challenge to succeed based on a preponderance of the evidence, while others might require a heightened showing. . . . The result could well be that a single candidate would be declared ineligible in some States, but not others, based on the same conduct (and perhaps even the same factual record).
>
> . . . An evolving electoral map could dramatically change the behavior of voters, parties, and States across the country, in different ways and at different times. The disruption would be all the more acute—and could nullify the votes of

millions and change the election result—if Section 3 enforcement were attempted after the Nation has voted. . . . Nothing in the Constitution requires that we endure such chaos—arriving at any time or different times, up to and perhaps beyond the Inauguration.[34]

This concern about "chaos" links *Trump v. Anderson* with *Trump v. United States*, and helps identify the intensely pragmatic foundations of decisions that purport to be founded on strictly legal materials.[35] Because *Trump v. United States* barely scratches the surfaces of those materials in renovating the law of presidential immunity, it might well be fair to regard it as founded not on law, strictly speaking, but on a commitment to (what the justices take to be) a form of judicial statesmanship. That form of statesmanship was designed to protect the separation of powers. The problem is that it turned out to make hash of it.

For those who insist on fidelity to the legal sources, the most charitable verdict on *Trump v. United States* is Scottish: Not proven. For those who are favorably disposed toward judicial statesmanship, a degree of skepticism is also in order. The parade of horribles, signaled by the idea of a self-cannibalizing executive branch, is met by another (and far worse) parade of horribles, signaled by an immensely powerful president who is, for the first time in US history, broadly free from the operations of criminal law. Allowing that kind of president is inconsistent with the highest aspirations of the system of separation of powers.

6   THE MOST DANGEROUS BRANCH

If public officials are going to resolve national problems, they must have access to a great deal of information, much of it highly technical. Of the three branches of the national government, the executive is by far the most knowledgeable, not only in foreign affairs but also in the domestic domain. It is also, and partly for that reason, the most dangerous.

One reason is that it combines immensely superior knowledge, or access to knowledge, with something else: massive powers of initiative. Those powers can be exercised for good or for evil. None of this was adequately anticipated at the time of the founding.

The informational advantage of the executive continues to grow every year. In particular, the disparity between the knowledge of the executive branch and the knowledge of Congress is increasing. Because Congress gets to make the law, it does have an upper hand; as we have seen, the executive usually cannot act unless Congress authorizes it to act. But when the executive branch and Congress are in conflict, it is a bit of a mismatch, because the executive branch knows so much more. Congress has also authorized the executive branch to do all sorts of things, and the president—and those who work for him—can move quickly and sometimes even immediately.

The first months of every administration make the point very clear. The beginning of the presidency of Joe Biden is a clear example. The beginning of the presidency of Donald Trump is a spectacularly clear example. If a president wants to uproot the current system, he can do that. If a president wants to uproot the system of separation of powers, he might be able to do that too.

Judges also face an informational deficit, and much of the time, they simply do not know what they do not know. The distorting prism of litigation often makes that deficit in knowledge less than fully visible to judges, who are hearing from mere translators in the form of lawyers. These lawyers may not even speak the real language of the underlying dispute, especially in cases that involve highly technical matters: What are the risks posed by mercury? What is the best way to reduce the threat of salmonella in meat and poultry products? Judges have a tough time answering such questions. They do not know enough.

THE DEEP STATE

President Donald Trump has often complained about the "deep state," but it is a big help to any president. Actually, it is essential. Within the executive branch, there are numerous specialists, many of whom have spent years or even decades doing concentrated work on particular subjects: aviation, carcinogens, immigration, genetically modified organisms, pandemics, and more. On serious questions, such specialists bring their knowledge to bear. They work for political appointees, but they are not themselves political; they labor across administrations, sometimes for decades.

Those within the executive branch also have managerial responsibilities, which similarly entail possession of a great deal of information. They know how to get things done. They know how to set priorities. If you tell them what to achieve, they can achieve it. At least when things are working well, they tend to see how various substantive areas and questions relate to one another, and which deserve attention first.

If officials do not proceed on one task, their inaction might, in the abstract, seem objectionable or even scandalous. It might be exactly that! But the inaction might not be a product of neglect or dereliction, but rather of scarce resources and a belief that other tasks deserve priority. The real question might involve timing, and those in the executive branch are in a unique position to see why (and how) timing is important. For example, an issue that appears to be neglected in one year might, in reality, be subject to at least a general plan and might receive careful attention two years later (and that could be according to plan). The executive branch might also know that one apparent policy priority is, on reflection, not nearly as pressing. Pursuing it might even pose a serious risk of unintended adverse consequences.

Moreover, a problem that concerns many people (including legislators and litigants) might not even be serious, in the sense that it does not pose significant risks in the real world. Their concern might be a product of well-organized private groups, anecdotes, or generalized suspicion of some entity (e.g., "polluters" or "the banks" or "radical environmentalists"). Government faces a constant bandwidth problem, and observers—focused on just one of many issues—suffer from "bandwidth neglect." There is a big downside. It is also true that the executive can focus its attention on ten problems and not a hundred problems, and the ninety problems that it is neglecting might be really serious.

The legislative branch also suffers from a bandwidth problem, and it is at least as acute. It also leads in unfortunate directions: not toward management of multiple problems, usually overseen by genuine specialists immersed in the details, but far more often toward an insistent focus on narrow political concerns and the concerns of the day, often voiced by powerful interests or raised by a newspaper story. Within the legislative branch, the sheer press of time and electoral incentives often lead to dependence on interest groups, headlines, cable news, social media, and "talking points," which, in turn, ensures serious informational deficits. When members of Congress see incompetence or wrongdoing or call for someone's resignation, they might be right—but they might also have no idea what they are talking about.

Judges face their own challenges. Though they typically have a lot more time, and hence less intense bandwidth issues, their information is partial and fragmentary, sometimes a kind of cartoon. It is a product of the adversary process, run by lawyers, which can lead to distorted and wildly inadequate perspectives. Judges cannot possibly have an adequate sense of the full range of issues with which executive officials must deal. Judges will sometimes be presented with, and convinced by, a narrative of executive indifference or overreaching, even if that narrative has little or no resemblance to reality. All this bears on the real world of the separation of powers.

On purely epistemic grounds, there is special reason for deference to the decisions of the most knowledgeable branch. It makes sense to defer to those who know the most, certainly on questions of fact. But here, as elsewhere, general propositions do not decide concrete cases. The motives and competence of executive branch officials cannot always be trusted. (You might have noticed that.) The executive branch might itself be influenced by interest groups. Its own perspective might be skewed. It might fail to respect liberty.

There is a particular problem of "happy talk," by which such officials, attempting to please or calm the president in particular, present a rosy view of situations in a way that produces erroneous decisions. In my time in the executive branch under Presidents Obama and Biden, I saw plenty of happy talk, in which the president's advisers told him that all was well, even though it wasn't. I have referred to a separate problem: Engaged in conversation with one another, members of the executive branch might fall victim to *group polarization*, by which people end up more confident, more unified, and more extreme simply because they are talking with one another. That happens a lot.

It is also true that not every executive branch, or every topic in every executive branch, is the same. Sometimes the executive branch is highly professional; sometimes it really isn't. Some issues trigger dogmas. If people begin with strong antecedent convictions, the informational advantages of the executive branch are much less important. If the president thinks that a halt to immigration is an excellent idea, even though the evidence suggests otherwise, then the executive branch will support a proposal that cannot be justified by evidence. It is true, as we have seen, that courts and Congress can provide valuable checks: in the case of the former, consistency with law, and in the case of the latter, indispensable authorization and limitations.

Nonetheless, the informational advantages of the executive branch are an essential part of thinking about the contemporary system of separation of powers. These advantages were not clearly visible until relatively recently, and they bear directly on a wide range of questions involving the allocation of authority. They also show what Americans have most to fear.

WHO KNOWS WHAT?

Suppose that a branch of government, acting in accordance with its distinctive role, is trying to decide whether to regulate mercury and ozone; whether to require graphic warnings on cigarette packages; whether to impose caps on late fees from credit card companies; how to respond to the problem of distracted driving; whether to ban ozone-depleting chemicals from asthma medicines; or whether to require trucks to be equipped with improved brakes. In each of these cases, the government needs to assemble a great deal of information about the likely consequences.

It might be the case, for example, that at low levels, mercury and ozone present serious public health risks—or, instead, tiny ones. Graphic warnings may or may not turn out to be highly effective. Caps on late fees might lead credit card companies not to give credit cards to risky applicants. Bans on ozone-depleting chemicals from asthma medicines may or may not have significant adverse effects on asthma patients. In all these cases, people might differ with respect to values, and those differences might well affect their ultimate judgments. Some people do have strong, immediate, value-driven reactions to words like *ozone* and *mercury*. As one high-level public official with strong environmentalist leanings once told me in government, "mercury is nasty stuff."

But consider another possibility: On a host of issues (certainly not all!), the real differences between people involve the facts, and when people genuinely understand the facts, they will often agree on what to do, *whatever their values may be*. If ozone presents serious health risks at low levels in the ambient air, and if the costs associated with reducing those risks are not high, then it would be hard to argue against regulations that would reduce those risks. And if ozone presents tiny risks at low levels, and if the costs associated with producing those low levels are in the many billions of dollars, the argument for regulations that would produce those low levels seems weak. After a certain demonstration of facts, differences of values often turn out to be far less relevant than they first seem.

Of course, it is true that values affect people's assessments of the facts. People's reasoning is sometimes *motivated*, especially on high-level political issues. In Washington and elsewhere (but maybe Washington in particular), judgments about the effects of environmental regulations, health care policies, and immigration reform frequently reflect, or are decisively influenced by, people's antecedent political convictions. This point might seem obvious, but it should be underlined and put in bold letters because it is such a serious and pervasive obstacle to agreement and progress. It also bears on possible mistakes by the executive branch—and the legislative branch too. It helps justify the system of separation of powers.

Those who are inclined to favor environmental regulation tend to think that the benefits of such regulation are very high (and typically understated) and that the costs are low (and typically overstated). Those inclined to reject environmental regulation tend to think the opposite! In their view, agencies systematically overestimate the benefits and underestimate the costs. For many politically contested issues, judgments about facts are highly predictable: *If you know people's values, you will know what they think about disputed questions of fact.* Although this is beyond unfortunate, it is true and perhaps inevitable, at least for some actors and some institutions. One reason is that their incentives, and their sources of information, are not ambiguous. They learn from those they know and trust.

It is also true that some debates cannot be resolved by knowing the facts; they really do depend on values. For example, some people would oppose gun control restrictions, torture, or capital punishment even if they could be convinced that such practices might save lives. People might agree that an air pollution rule would save two hundred lives annually while also costing $1.5 billion but disagree about whether it is worth proceeding. As a cabinet official once asked me, "How do you put a price on a human life?" When facts are conclusive, it is not because values are irrelevant, but instead because there is a sufficient consensus on them. Sometimes there is no such consensus, leading to intractable disagreement even when no factual question is at issue.

But the broader point remains: More than we tend to think, the central political debates in the United States, Europe, and elsewhere turn, above all, on the facts. If the facts can be sorted out and agreed on, the likelihood of disagreement will diminish dramatically. In nations that are intensely polarized along political lines, citizens greatly underestimate the extent to which a consensus on the consequences of a policy can eliminate seemingly intractable disagreements over whether it should be pursued. If increases in the minimum wage lead to dramatic decreases in employment, would it really make sense to favor them? If banning inhalers emitting ozone-depleting substances would seriously harm asthma sufferers without having significant environmental benefits, who would argue in favor of such bans?

Here is the central point: With respect to the acquisition of information, the executive branch is usually in a far better position than the legislative and judicial branches. It has a massive stock of specialists, often operating in teams, and the teams often know a ton. Some of those specialists have spent many years studying and working on the subject. Of course, the executive branch's capacity to obtain information is far from perfect, but most of the time, the executive branch knows incalculably more than other branches—and when it does not know something, it is in an excellent position to find out. I will defend these claims shortly, but let us now turn to some of the weaknesses of the other two branches.

JUDGES AND LAWYERS

For the judiciary, a big problem is that judges cannot acquire information on their own. They must depend on arguments and briefs and, hence, on advocates. Judges might be terrifically smart, but in any case that involves issues like those sketched earlier, the judges' knowledge will inevitably be partial. This problem is compounded by the fact that judges are generalists who usually lack specialized knowledge of technical areas.

True, some judges are specialists, and when they are not, they might be able to obtain some mastery of an area. But even when they are specialists, their own understanding of a particular problem is likely to be limited simply because they must depend on advocates. And because advocates are self-interested, clever, and often superb with rhetoric, they will present judges with highly stylized and distorted pictures of reality. Lawyers who challenge executive action will suggest that there has been an important omission or confusion, when in fact the relevant issue has received sustained internal attention for days, weeks, or even months. Because of the distorting prism of litigation, judges may never be made aware of that fact.

Here's a little secret: Those who have worked in both Republican and Democratic administrations are frequently stunned to see how often judges seize on some apparently weak argument, carefully considered by multiple officials in technical (not political) terms, and then invoke that argument to invalidate executive action. The judges seem to think that executive officials were negligent or "captured," when nothing could be further from the truth. Ignorant of the process, judges are convinced by an argument that clever lawyers (self-interested and, in a deep sense, clueless) were able to make convincing. Sometimes, of course, the judges are right.

It is relevant that litigation focuses judges on a single case or dispute, when proper resolution often requires an understanding of a broader canvas. For example, an agency's apparent slowness in proceeding on one rule, or in one area, might seem to suggest sloth or indifference, when it is actually a product of careful priority setting—something that is not readily visible to judges. There may be no neglect at all, but simply an effort to produce sensible management.

To be sure, the executive will often be a party to litigation, and it can try to provide judges with the information that it has. The problem—and it is a serious and insufficiently appreciated one—is that in litigation, the executive consists of *lawyers*. They are not scientists or economists, and their understanding of both science and economics will be incomplete. Like judges, they are generalists. They might be adequate, better than average, or even sensational. But in many respects, they serve as mere translators. They will usually be latecomers to the problem, and what they know will reflect what they learn from others.

Regardless of how intelligent and hardworking lawyers are, their own knowledge is likely to be partial and fragmentary, at least compared to that held by those who are involved in making actual decisions within the executive branch. They will do the best they can, but they are very unlikely to have the kinds of knowledge that come from genuine involvement in the underlying decisions. Judges take the lawyers as representing and speaking for the executive branch, as they are, but there is a large difference between a spokesperson (like an official in a communications office) and a genuine decision-maker who was actually involved.

Here is the worst part: In any case worthy of the name, good adversaries will be able to identify two, three, or perhaps even a dozen apparently reasonable objections to a decision by executive branch officials. They might be able to produce considerable alarm and even outrage. How could such officials have been so stupid? Were they captured by interest groups? Were they overzealous? Driven by ideology? But much of the time, *every one of those objections will have been carefully considered within the executive branch, often for many hours of substantive discussion by many people.*

Still, that is no guarantee, of course, that the executive will have gotten it right. Its officials might indeed be biased, confused, negligent, incompetent, political in a bad sense, or suffering from motivated reasoning. As we shall see, the executive branch contains built-in safeguards against all of these risks. But these safeguards are imperfect, and a poorly functioning executive branch can override them. That is one reason that the most knowledgeable branch is also the most dangerous.

CONGRESS AND ELECTIONS

In theory, of course, Congress can obtain its own information by holding hearings or consulting experts. But members of Congress are also generalists, their staffs are relatively small, and they have to focus on reelection. Usually, they don't know a whole lot. When they are described as "experts"—on environmental issues, health care, or foreign policy—it might be true, but it might also be hyperbolic. Within Congress, members are usually experts at one thing: doing what it takes to get reelected. In terms of substantive issues, they tend to lack the bandwidth to become experts. Of course, there are exceptions, but that is the general rule. Committee chairs or committee members often spend many hours on a general topic, but when it comes to particular issues, there is a real chance that their knowledge will be fragmentary simply because of the multiple demands on their time, their incentives, their role, and their limited sources of information.

I saw this repeatedly in my various stints in Washington. Working for the executive branch, I was surrounded by people who devoted months or years to specific problems. They might be wrong, but they knew a ton. Members of Congress were often extremely impressive, and they were certainly quick studies. Some of them knew much more than anyone had a right to expect. But most of them knew far less than those in the executive branch, because they were generalists. They had broad values, and important information, but most of the time, they did not know much about the details.

At least it is usually true that members of Congress, even those with years of experience, lack the specific and detailed knowledge of those within the executive branch who deal with the same questions. I have acknowledged that some members are exceptions, but consider a comparative question: Who knows more on a particular substantive topic, the most informed member of Congress or, say, the administrator of the National Highway Traffic Safety Administration, or the assistant attorney general for civil rights? The answer is almost always the latter, not least because members of the executive branch have large staffs on whose expertise they can draw.

We can see this point when members of Congress ask questions during hearings. Those questions are frequently a result of very recent briefing from their staffs, perhaps given shortly before the hearing itself. Sometimes members will not have much information about the topic at hand; they might even read the questions, prepared by their staff, without fully having a grasp on them. If they press a member of the executive branch to answer a question—about, for example, an enforcement policy, a health care regulation, or immigration—members of Congress will almost always lack the background of the witness, who might well have spent numerous hours on the problem.

They may make serious accusations, and they may be entirely sincere in doing so, but the accusations may or may not be justified. (Sometimes they lack any justification, though sometimes they are right.) When their base of knowledge is thin, members will often be unable to ask decent follow-up questions. And even when their base of knowledge is thick—even when they are, in a sense, genuine experts on the underlying questions, having spent considerable time on them—they will have far less information than the witness from the executive branch.

It is important to take these points as descriptive and general rather than as criticisms or objections. We are speaking of the real world of the separation of powers. The knowledge of public officials is a product of their distinctive roles and accompanying constraints. Like judges, members of Congress are generalists, and even more than judges, the pressures on their time are enormous. An executive branch official can draw on the expertise of public servants who have spent years on the problem of highway safety or the situation in Egypt. A member of Congress cannot easily do the same; congressional staffs, many of whom focus in significant part on politics and electoral considerations, are unlikely to have an equivalent stock of knowledge. Their knowledge might be impressively wide, but it is not usually deep.

Above all, the insistent focus on politics and reelection has four major effects. First, it makes it far more difficult for members to focus on complex or technical questions. The result is that they must resort to simple heuristics, or mental shortcuts. These are not "simple heuristics that make us smart"; they are instead "simple heuristics that make us polarized," and they are far too unidimensional to capture reality. A common example: "If the EPA is for it, I am against it." A more common example: "If the president is for it, I am for it too." Yet another: "I agree with the labor unions." One more: "The National Association of Manufacturers is usually right."

Second, electoral pressures can make short-term political calculations highly salient or even decisive, pressing members' decisions in particular directions and making the acquisition of complex or technical information far less important. In other words, members of Congress lack the incentive to acquire that information. If reelection will be eased or facilitated if a member announces his view that a new immigration initiative is a terrible idea, then it will be singularly difficult for that member to endorse a new immigration initiative, or even to remain silent on it. And what is the point of becoming an expert on the new immigration initiative? There are undoubtedly many cases in which a member takes a position not because she has a serious commitment to it, but because she believes that she must if she seeks to retain her job. For example, when I was seeking confirmation by the United States Senate in 2009, one prominent senator told me that he strongly supported me but would of course vote against me. (It was a very cordial conversation.)

Third, the need to focus on reelection, especially when accompanied by the sheer press of time, increases the risk of influence by—and, on occasion, even near-exclusive attention to—information provided by private groups with clear commitments to one or another course of action. Reliance on that information may be a product of a simple heuristic, to the effect that certain groups are likely to be right (e.g., the AFL-CIO heuristic, the Natural Resources Defense Council heuristic, the Federalist Society heuristic, or the National Association of Manufacturers heuristic). A Democrat in the House of Representatives might simply channel the views of labor unions or a well-respected environmental organization. A Republican Senator might repeat the concerns of coal companies in a particular area.

Talking points will matter greatly. They might well end up being determinative. Within the executive branch, of course, talking points are also important, especially when officials are speaking with the media. Officials are usually given a set of talking points and asked to stick closely to them. But in actual policy discussions—as opposed to communications events— talking points are almost always irrelevant. The questions involve the substance, and talking points are just a hindrance.

Within the legislative branch, there is of course nothing necessarily nefarious or untoward here. Again, time is short, and members are busy, with numerous issues to which to attend. Reliance on the views of trusted others might be the best available strategy—certainly if reelection is the goal, and perhaps also if the goal is to make the right decisions.

Consider a small example: When I was administrator of the Office of Information and Regulatory Affairs (OIRA), I testified on a number of occasions before Senate and House committees. On one of those occasions, I was asked about a report from the Heritage Foundation, which purported to show an explosion, on my watch, of regulatory costs. An explosion of costs is not something to be proud of! This was a pretty strong accusation.

In the upper right-hand corner, the report contained the words *talking points* and then listed them. Asked about the report, I noted, with what I thought was some humor and wryness, that I had learned that in Washington that if a report has the words *talking points* in a prominent place, it is not necessarily objective. No one in the room smiled. In fact, no one in the room seemed to have any idea what I was talking about. Did they think I was offering a talking point?

Fourth, the focus on reelection tends to make political considerations the coin of the realm, so that it is not so simple to think of substantive issues in nonpolitical terms. Instead of asking about the costs and benefits of a regulation designed to increase safety in the workplace, someone might ask, "What does the Chamber of Commerce think?" Within the executive branch, it is easy to identify, almost immediately, people "with Capitol Hill experience," because they think so readily in political terms. Such experience is of course invaluable. With respect to the operations of the legislative branch, and how to allay concerns or to promote interest or enthusiasm, those with such experience know far more than people who lack it.

I do not mean to say that members of Congress do not engage with the substance. Many of them do so. (I single out Senator James Lankford from Oklahoma, who always knows what he is talking about, and who has extraordinary integrity and decency.) The only point is that much of the time, their minds tend to go readily to interest groups and polls, and less readily to real-world consequences or substantive issues. They have an epistemic advantage in the sense that they know how to "work the hill," but when it comes to policy, they usually have serious epistemic disadvantages. They might not think in policy terms. Their ignorance is a problem, and it is also a weakness. It makes the executive branch more dangerous.

7 DELIBERATIVE DEMOCRACY IN THE TRENCHES

In chapter 1, we saw that the separation of powers was designed in large part to create a deliberative democracy. Can deliberative democracy be found *within* the executive branch? When things are working well, it can. Of course, the executive branch is accountable for its decisions and therefore subject to democratic constraints. These constraints often loom large, especially in the period right after an election ("What were our campaign promises?")—and right before as well, including the midterms, when no executive branch wants to undermine the efforts of members of the president's own party, much less "lose the House."

But let's return to the deep state. As I have emphasized, there are numerous experts within any cabinet-level department. They have been working on the relevant issues for many years and through multiple administrations. They do not care at all about elections, politics, or interest groups. To be sure, they might well have their own biases. They might be mired in, and wedded to, existing practices. They might be, and often are, resistant to significant change, on the theory that things have always been done a certain way. They tend to be Burkeans, supportive of traditions. They might suffer from an acute form of status quo bias. But again, they also have an immense stock of knowledge. With respect to deliberation, the central point is that they will also be working and exchanging facts and views with numerous other people within the executive branch, at least on the most significant questions. For multiple questions, this process of interagency collaboration is formalized and routinized.

REALITY

With respect to both domestic and international affairs, it typically takes something like the following (highly stylized) form, at least under most presidents: Some kind of interagency process includes representatives of various parts of the government, who work together on some issue, whether short term (in need of resolution within, say, three weeks) or long term (not requiring resolution for many months). Sometimes their discussions take months or more, and they have a degree of intensity and animation. Diverse people, with different knowledge and perspectives, are frequently involved. For example, there might be participants from the National Economic Council, the Council of Economic Advisers, the Office of Management and Budget, the Department of the Treasury, the Department of State, and the Department of Energy. They might be "policy" officials, meaning people who have some connection to the incumbent administration, some of whom might have been confirmed by the Senate. But those officials will be staffed and assisted by people without any evident political affiliation; they are specialists and technocrats.

After they are done, they might be able to resolve the issue, or it might be "elevated" to some kind of "deputies' committee," consisting of, for example, the deputy secretary of state, the deputy secretary of defense, the deputy secretary of energy, and the deputy director of the Office of Management and Budget, who might, as the highest-ranking official within the Executive Office of the President, run the meeting. After that, the issue might be resolved, or it might be elevated to a "principals' committee," which will consist of cabinet-level officials. The principals' committee might be able to resolve the question, but at that stage, or thereafter, the question might go to the president. If the issue is a very important one, the principals' committee might be chaired by one of the highest-ranking officials in the White House—perhaps the national security adviser or the chief of staff, who is usually, next to the president, the most important person within the executive branch of the government.

Stylized and brief though it is, this account should be sufficient to show that within the executive branch, there is a great deal of deliberation, and it often involves people with diverse perspectives and high levels of technical expertise. Everyone works for the president, of course, which stifles debate. Still, there may be a high level of heterogeneity and disagreement that has to be worked through, typically as a result of substantive exchanges, with a high premium on the acquisition of relevant information.

To take an example with which I am familiar: In 2009–2010, an interagency working group produced a "social cost of carbon," meaning the economic cost of a ton of carbon emissions suitable for use in regulatory impact analyses. The group included representatives of the Council of Economic Advisers, the Council on Environmental Quality, the Department of Agriculture, the Department of Commerce, the Department of Energy, the Department of Transportation, the Environmental Protection Agency, the National Economic Council, the Office of Energy and Climate Change, the Office of Management and Budget, the Office of Science and Technology Policy, and the Department of the Treasury. Members of this group, like members of countless others, had different information and, in government jargon, different *equities*, meaning institutional interests associated with their office or department, or their *building*.

The EPA, for example, is inevitably a crucially important participant in discussions of the social cost of carbon and sees environmental protection as its major concern, while the Department of Commerce seeks to promote commercial activity. The Department of Energy has a great deal of expertise on the effects of carbon emissions and the science as a whole, and the Council of Economic Advisers has expertise on such economic issues as the appropriate discount rate. The result involved the aggregation of a great deal of scientific, economic, and legal expertise, with agreements being forged through substantive arguments. Notably for this decision, politics— understood as electoral considerations or possible press reactions—did not play the slightest role. The discussions were highly technical and involved the substance of the matter. Of course, different administrations take different approaches, and a top-down instruction (from, say, President Joe Biden or President Donald Trump) can resolve issues that would otherwise be debated.

REGULATION

With respect to the regulatory process, the system of internal review takes a somewhat different, but also highly formalized, form. Suppose that the EPA wishes to issue a new national ambient air quality standard involving ozone. If the regulation is submitted to OIRA (and it certainly would have to be), it will be scrutinized by numerous offices within the Executive Office of the President, including the Office of Management and Budget, the Domestic Policy Council, the National Economic Council, the Council of Economic Advisers, the Office of the Vice President, and the Office of the Chief of Staff. If it has international implications, it will also be scrutinized by the Department of State, the National Security Council, and the Office of the United States Trade Representative. Within the Executive Office of the President, the initial comments will come from staff, not from high-level officials or anyone concerned with politics. The principal focus will be substantive rather than political. At the early stages, political consider-ations are not likely to be raised at all.

Draft rules, both proposed and final, are also subject to scrutiny by other departments within the executive branch. If a regulation has implications for the energy supply, it will be assessed by the Department of Energy. The Departments of Commerce and Treasury might well be involved, especially if the regulation raises economic issues. To the extent that there are labor implications, the Department of Labor will comment, and what it says will likely matter. If agriculture is affected, the Department of Agriculture will comment as well. The Department of the Interior might well be involved. Within the agencies, technical analysts typically undertake the initial review. They will be civil servants, specialists in the issues at hand.

This process of scrutiny is often intense. Issues of policy and law might receive detailed attention. Perhaps people disagree. Perhaps there will be legal objections from lawyers within the Department of the Treasury. Per-haps someone in the Department of Energy will suggest that some of the policy choices are wrong. Perhaps the economic analysis will be seen by someone in the Council of Economic Advisers to contain a serious mistake. Any analysis of benefits and costs will probably be seen and scrutinized by numerous people in different places within the executive branch.

Frequently, issues and concerns can be worked out at the staff level after extended, substantive discussion. OIRA will convene staff-level discussions in which most of the issues can be resolved, whether they involve econom-ics, policy, or law. But here as well, issues might be "elevated." For example, an assistant secretary of one department might engage with the assistant secretary at the rulemaking agency and with OIRA's deputy administrator to explore interagency concerns. Sometimes the issue will be raised to the OIRA administrator himself. If (and this is rare) agreement is not possible

at that level, then further discussions will be required, with ultimate resolution by a group of principals or (in a very rare case) by the president
personally.

Importantly, the regulatory process is not only an internal one; it also
involves citizens, not merely public officials. For regulations, public comment is frequently involved, and it can make a large difference. In most
administrations, OIRA's institutional inclination—and it is a strong one—is
to make clear that comments are invited on a wide range of choices in
a proposed rule, and that they are also invited on alternatives to those
choices. Agencies often think, and OIRA often urges them to think, that
their own judgments are provisional and that the role of the comment
process is to learn whether or not they are right. For that learning to occur,
the public must be urged to comment on the provisional choices and on
alternatives to them.

LEARNING

It is not much of a stretch to see the inspiration for this form of deliberative
democracy in Friedrich Hayek, and especially his emphasis on the dispersed
nature of knowledge in society. Of course (and to say the least), Hayek was
not a great fan of the modern regulatory state, but his work on widely
dispersed information has helped inspire the effort to go outside of government and learn from what others know.

When things are working well, one reason for the great length of final
rules is that their preambles engage with comments, frequently in considerable detail. And in many cases, public comments help produce substantial
changes. Sometimes agencies learn that their proposals need to be with-
drawn. Sometimes they learn that a fundamentally different approach,
one that saves costs, is best. Sometimes they learn that a more expansive
approach, which increases benefits, is justified. A great deal of deliberation
thus occurs between public officials and citizens, not only as a result of
meetings, but also, and perhaps most fundamentally, through the process
of public comment. Different administrations of course look different, and
what happens might not live up to the very highest ideals, but much of the
time, it is worthy of the idea of deliberative democracy.

These points suggest strong reasons to reject the view, offered energeti-
cally by some law professors, that courts should be less willing to defer

to executive action when that action is a product not of the autonomous decision-making of the rulemaking agency involved, but of numerous officials within the executive branch. Put to one side the fact that courts will not ordinarily know about the internal process of deliberation or be able to sort out the precise role of various officials. The much deeper problem is that this view has things *exactly backward*. If an agency is acting on its own, there might well be reason to worry about myopia, mission orientation, and tunnel vision, potentially compromising the ultimate judgment. If multiple officials are involved, there are of course no guarantees, but the risks are reduced because of the safeguards provided by diverse perspectives. The case for judicial deference to executive action is far stronger if the action is supported and produced by numerous officials, not just by the rulemaking agency.

With respect to law, there is a supporting fact, based on my own experience: general counsels within agencies are usually excellent, but in at least some cases, their legal judgments are influenced by the substantive goals and hopes of their own cabinet secretaries. Lawyers in other parts of government—the Department of Justice, the White House Counsel's Office, the Office of Management and Budget's General Counsel, other agencies— may have greater objectivity even if they have less specialized expertise. Lawyers outside of the rulemaking agency often have more distance from the agency's political mission and are sometimes more reliable on the underlying law. What is true of legal issues can be true of policy questions as well, including predictions of likely consequences, such as costs and benefits, for which economists at the Council of Economic Advisers might be more reliable than economists at rulemaking agencies.

TOO ROSY

The picture that I have presented is an idealized one. Although it sometimes matches reality (at least in my experience), not every executive branch, and not every issue in the same executive branch, is the same. There is an elephant in the room, and it is the second term of President Donald Trump: In 2025, at least, the sheer speed and aggressiveness of presidential action suggests that we are not speaking of an intensely deliberative process.

With that example in mind, some people will be deeply skeptical about any picture of the executive branch as embodying an appealing form of deliberative democracy. Others will point to their own preferred examples—real or imagined—in which it seems misleading, incomplete, or worse to depict the branch in this light, or to neglect the extent to which political judgments and political biases, and sheer cluelessness, can dwarf knowledge of facts. The examples may or may not be good ones, depending as they do on incomplete information, and examples are no more than that. But they do illustrate a more general problem, at least in some domains. It is easy to find or to envision other administrations, past, present, or future, that draw my characterization into serious doubt.

To put the point most vividly: How realistic would that characterization seem if the president is or were X, where X is one's least favorite possibility? (Some people see Donald Trump as X.) Maybe X has terrible but fixed convictions and is unwilling to listen to reason. Maybe X does not much care about the facts. Maybe X does not care about public comments. Maybe X is unduly influenced by well-organized interest groups.

During a Republican administration many years ago, I sent some suggestions about how to deal with climate change to a high-level public official, who was (and is) a committed conservative as well as a technical expert and was (and is) also a good friend. My suggested approach would not have imposed high costs. I was puzzled to receive no answer (though after my own experience in government, learning about the potential risks of using email, my puzzlement dissipated). When I saw him at the White House, he came right up to me and said, "Cass, your suggestion isn't bad at all, but you have absolutely no idea how conservative my colleagues are!"

Note, however, that even if the president were X, some decisions of the executive branch would not be affected at all. Some such decisions would be relatively routine (even if important), and they would be settled reasonably—even under X. But it must be acknowledged that if the president were X, or anyone like X, the epistemic advantages of the executive branch would matter much less, at least on high-profile questions, where relevant interest groups might be able to exert their influence or where the antecedent convictions of the president and his high-level officials might be ridiculously fixed and firm. That is a key reason that the executive branch is the most dangerous branch of the law.

Let's be concrete. If such officials believe that climate change is a myth, or not worth attention, then technical experts within the executive branch are likely to have a hard time establishing the social cost of carbon. If the president or high-level officials favor very stringent regulation of ozone, mercury, and particulate matter—whatever the facts show—then decisions will not reflect the epistemic advantages of the executive branch. If such officials are enthusiastic about renewable fuels and want to maximize their use—whatever the facts show—then it is useless to emphasize that executive branch officials have unique access to information.

It must therefore be acknowledged that the arguments I am making here depend on the assumption that most of the time, the executive branch operates as if it were not run by X. I believe that this has usually been true under both Democratic and Republican presidents, certainly outside of the context of the most politicized questions (and, frequently enough, in that context as well). But it must be acknowledged that under any president, the risk of stupid decision-making is well above zero, and the influence of interest groups cannot be discounted. If the president really were X, then the picture I have offered here would not be realistic.

KNOWLEDGE AND CONSTRAINT

Institutional questions cannot be resolved in the abstract. As we saw in chapter 1, some system of judicial review is foundational to the American system of public law, but the argument for its existence depends on a set of contingent assumptions. There is no abstract or a priori justification for the American system of judicial review (though I like it a lot).

In a hypothetical and unrealistic (but not unimaginable) world, the most knowledgeable branch should proceed on its own and without much in the way of judicial constraint. Suppose, for example, that the most knowledgeable branch were expert in the law as well as everything else and that it was most unlikely to proceed arbitrarily. Suppose that judges' judgments were highly unreliable with respect to law, including in their review of the exercise of discretion. On those assumptions, judicial review would not be a good idea.

Our constitutional order, of course, rejects these assumptions, and for excellent reasons. Notwithstanding what I have said here, there is a serious risk that the judgments of the executive branch, influenced by its own policy preferences, will be erroneous, self-aggrandizing, self-serving, or out of control. To the extent that they are not, it is in significant part because the courts are available to contest their legal judgments. My own experience in

government was that the prospect of judicial review was a powerful con-
straining force. The risk of unlawful action would be far higher without it.
If the courts were unavailable, there is no doubt that the rule of law and
liberty itself would be at a serious risk. Courts are not democratic branches,
but they safeguard democracy.

I have noted that within the executive branch, many perspectives are
available, but the fact remains that everyone works for a single person, which
will reduce the level of heterogeneity. Recall the problem of "happy talk."
Democratic administrations do not usually have a lot of Republicans in high
positions, and vice versa—and so, at times, strong challenges of the kind
that members of an opposing party might make are pretty much absent.

Recall chapter 2: If Congress must authorize the executive to act, that is a
built-in constraint on the exercise of national power. That constraint makes
the most sense if, as is plainly the case, the most knowledgeable branch
cannot always be trusted and might turn out to be dangerous. It also makes
sense if we insist that a degree of authorization, from diverse elected officials
with their own values and concerns, is an important safeguard of liberty.

8 THE GRAND NARRATIVE

"The dissent would permit Congress to concentrate the roles of prosecutor, judge, and jury in the hands of the Executive Branch. That is the very opposite of the separation of powers that the Constitution demands."[1]
—*SEC v. Jarkesy*, 144 S. Ct. 2117, 2139 (2024)

"The rise of administrative bodies probably has been the most significant legal trend of the last century and perhaps more values today are affected by their decisions than by those of all the courts, review of administrative decisions apart. They also have begun to have important consequences on personal rights. They have become a veritable fourth branch of the Government, which has deranged our three-branch legal theories much as the concept of a fourth dimension unsettles our three-dimensional thinking."[2]
—*FTC v. Ruberoid Co.*, 343 U.S. 470, 487 (1952) (Jackson, J., dissenting)

For many decades, American law and politics have been haunted by a Grand Narrative.[3]

The Grand Narrative points to three transgressions of the separation of powers, in the form of successive breaches of Article I, Article II, and Article III of the Constitution, all occurring in the first half of the twentieth century and motivated in part by the New Deal.[4] (So we are really speaking of three Grand Narratives, subsumed under one.) The Grand Narrative is the best way to understand a host of developments in American administrative law. Those developments are an effort to restore a (perceived) status quo ante, in the form of an insistence on the (perceived) requirements of the three articles. That insistence has implications, at least, for public law all over the world, including Canada and Europe.

Recall that Article I vests legislative power in "a Congress of the United States." According to the Grand Narrative, the grant of broad discretionary authority to the executive branch amounts to an impermissible transfer of legislative power.[5] After the New Deal and the Great Society, legislative power is broadly exercised by regulatory agencies.[6] It is true that in *Schechter Poultry*,[7] decided in 1935, the Supreme Court struck down a grant of open-ended authority, but the court has *never* used the nondelegation doctrine to strike down an act of Congress since that year. In view of the sheer breadth of discretionary power regularly given to agencies, those who believe in the Grand Narrative think that the court's forbearance is a palpable abdication of constitutional responsibilities. According to the Grand Narrative, the constitutional problem is that such agencies are effectively lawmakers: They have open-ended discretion to do as they wish and thus to make law. An additional problem is that they can issue binding rules, even though part of the definition of the legislative power, vested in Congress, is that it alone can issue binding rules.[8] In these various ways, the grant of discretionary authority to the executive branch violates the separation of powers.

As we have seen, Article II vests executive power in "a President of the United States." According to the Grand Narrative, the exercise of executive power by people who are free from plenary presidential control is impermissible.[9] The constitutional problem is that after the New Deal, the United States has seen the rise of a "headless fourth branch"[10] of government, consisting of independent officials operating without presidential supervision and essentially on their own: the National Labor Relations Board, the Securities and Exchange Commission, the Federal Trade Commission (FTC), the Federal Communications Commission, the Nuclear Regulatory Commission, the Federal Reserve Board, the Consumer Product Safety Commission, and many more. According to the Grand Narrative, these are constitutional barnacles, an institutional innovation foreign to the constitutional structure. Or perhaps they are constitutional parasites, burrowing from within to undermine fundamental constitutional commitments.

Article III vests judicial power "in one supreme Court, and in such inferior Courts as the Congress may from time to time ordain and establish."[11] Federal judges are given important protections of independence, and thus federal judges "shall hold their Offices during good Behavior, and shall, at stated Times, receive for their Services, a Compensation, which shall not be diminished during their Continuance in Office."[12] The constitutional problem is that after the New Deal, the United States has seen the rise of a large system of adjudication, or many systems of adjudication, consisting of judges who are not Article III judges.[13] All this, it is said, is a patent violation of the structural commitments embodied in Article III, sketched in chapters 2 and 3.[14]

According to the Grand Narrative, the situation is worse still. Administrative agencies do not merely exercise authorities in defiance of Articles I, II, and III. They also *combine* traditionally separated functions.[15] Many executive agencies do not merely execute the law; they also make it—and to make matters worse, they adjudicate. Many independent agencies do not only make law and adjudicate; to make matters worse, they also execute it, free from presidential control. Nothing in the Constitution permits all this.[16]

My purposes in this chapter are to outline the Grand Narrative, to establish its essential and mounting role in current administrative law, and to sketch what is wrong with it, in part by identifying competing narratives. In its current form, the Grand Narrative is an originalist narrative, but all or part of it might be wrong on originalist grounds, and originalism might be wrong. I aim to outline the Grand Narrative and to bring it to the surface, not to praise it (and candor compels an acknowledgement that, notwithstanding my enthusiasm for the separation of powers, I would prefer to bury it).

In saying that the approach sketched here is the Grand Narrative, I mean to emphasize its current centrality, not its validity. In the past, other separation of powers narratives counted as grand,[17] and something similar will almost certainly be true in the future.

ABDICATION

As the Grand Narrative has it, the New Deal was the defining period for the successive breaches of Articles I, II, and III, but things became much worse in the 1960s and 1970s, and there have been very bad moments since that time.[18] A central reason was capitulation, or abdication, by the Supreme Court. For Article II, *Humphrey's Executor*,[19] upholding the existence of independent agencies, is the defining decision, though a number of later rulings ratified and compounded the error.[20] For Article III, *Crowell v. Benson*,[21] allowing administrative adjudication, was the moment of constitutional abdication, though here too later rulings made a terrible thing even worse.[22] For Article I, no single decision stands out, but a series of rulings allowed Congress to grant open-ended discretion to agencies, so long as it provided an "intelligible principle"[23]—which need not be so intelligible, and which need not really count as a principle.[24]

We might see *American Trucking*[25] as the closest thing to *Humphrey's Executor* and *Crowell*, insofar as it can be read to say that "if Congress tells an agency to do whatever it thinks best, we will not stand in the way." In that case, the court upheld a seemingly broad grant of discretion: "requisite to protect the public health with an adequate margin of safety." The court did not much worry over whether that provision was unduly open-ended:

> In the history of the Court we have found the requisite "intelligible principle" lacking in only two statutes, one of which provided literally no guidance for the exercise of discretion, and the other of which conferred authority to regulate the entire economy on the basis of no more precise a standard than stimulating the economy by assuring "fair competition." We have, on the other hand, upheld the validity of § 11(b)(2) of the Public Utility Holding Company Act of 1935, 49 Stat. 821, which gave the Securities and Exchange Commission authority to modify the structure of holding company systems so as to ensure that they are not "unduly or unnecessarily complicate[d]" and do not "unfairly or inequitably distribute voting power among security holders." We have approved the wartime conferral of agency power to fix the prices of commodities at a level that "'will be generally fair and equitable and will effectuate the [in some respects conflicting] purposes of th[e] Act.'" And we have found an "intelligible principle" in various statutes authorizing regulation in the "public interest." In short, we have "almost never felt qualified to second-guess Congress regarding the permissible degree of policy judgment that can be left to those executing or applying the law."[26]

With these words, the court essentially gave the back of the hand to the view that Article I forbids Congress from giving broad discretion to the executive branch. A lot of people do not like that. They think that the court has ignored a plain constitutional imperative, central to the system of separation of powers.

For many decades, the Grand Narrative lurked in the shadows of American law—menacing, perhaps, but essentially harmless. It was a presence, a ghost, or perhaps a zombie (alive, kind of, but mostly dead). It might have been taught in law schools, but in the federal courts, the real action lay elsewhere—in more mundane kinds of things, such as challenges to agency action as arbitrary or capricious. Those who invoked the Grand Narrative were hardly silent, but they were marginalized. A nondelegation challenge to a federal statute was essentially doomed, the last refuge of scoundrels. *Humphrey's Executor* was settled law, and however narrowly it might have been understood when written, it was taken to remove constitutional doubts about independent agencies of multiple kinds.[27]

To be sure, there were continuing disputes about the relationship between Article III and agency adjudication, but they were at the margins and quite arcane.[28] For those who embraced the Grand Narrative, the fundamentals of administrative law had been settled, and settled quite wrongly. With respect to the separation of powers, the real Constitution was lost, or perhaps in exile.[29] That situation might have turned out to be stable and enduring.

THE GRAND NARRATIVE IN PRACTICE

But life is full of surprises. The Grand Narrative is now animating the largest developments in the field.

THE UNITARY EXECUTIVE

Turn now to Article II, where *Humphrey's Executor* is on the run. In two cases, the court seized on plausible but far-from-obvious distinctions to strike down statutes providing for agency independence—that is, for agencies operating independently of the president. In *Free Enterprise Fund*,[30] the court displayed grave dissatisfaction with the very idea of independent agencies. It began dramatically and in a way that introduced some central themes of the Grand Narrative:

> Our Constitution divided the "powers of the new Federal Government into three defined categories, Legislative, Executive, and Judicial." *INS v. Chadha*, 462 U. S. 919, 951 (1983). Article II vests "[t]he executive Power . . . in a President of the United States of America," who must "take Care that the Laws be faithfully executed." Art. II, § 1, cl. 1; id., § 3. In light of "[t]he impossibility that one man should be able to perform all the great business of the State," the Constitution provides for executive officers to "assist the supreme Magistrate in discharging the duties of his trust." 30 Writings of George Washington 334 (J. Fitzpatrick ed. 1939). Since 1789, the Constitution has been understood to empower the President to keep these officers accountable—by removing them from office, if necessary.[31]

Those ideas leave no room at all for independence: no room for an independent Federal Reserve Board, an independent Federal Communications Commission (FCC), an independent Securities and Exchange Commission (SEC). And though the court did not reject its precedents on that count, it was evidently uncomfortable with them. Pointedly and perhaps somewhat ominously, the court said this: "The parties do not ask us to reexamine any of these precedents, and we do not do so."[32]

Technically invalidating two layers of independence without questioning one, the court ruled that dual layers would compromise the president's authority under the Take Care Clause: "We hold that such multilevel protection from removal is contrary to Article II's vesting of the executive power in the President. The President cannot 'take Care that the Laws be faithfully executed' if he cannot oversee the faithfulness of the officers who execute them."[33] In *Free Enterprise Fund*, the court embraced a major part of the Grand Narrative.

In *Seila Law*,[34] the court held that while a multimember independent agency is constitutional, a single-headed commission is not. Thus the court struck down the statute creating the Consumer Financial Protection Bureau insofar as it granted independence to the bureau's director. A central part of the Grand Narrative appeared even more clearly there, for the court emphasized that Article II creates a strongly unitary executive branch: "Under our Constitution, the 'executive Power'—all of it—is 'vested in a President,' who must 'take Care that the Laws be faithfully executed.' Art. II, §1, cl. 1; id., §3. . . . The President's power to remove—and thus supervise—those who wield executive power on his behalf follows from the text of Article II, was settled by the First Congress, and was confirmed in the landmark decision *Myers v. United States*."[35]

In that short passage, the court plainly embraced the Grand Narrative with respect to Article II. In the court's view, the text of the Constitution creates a strongly unitary executive, giving the president unrestricted removal authority. That understanding was essentially settled by the Decision of 1789.[36] Any departure from the constitutional settlement is impermissible.

In embracing that understanding, the court dramatically limited its previous cases recognizing congressional authority to restrict the president's removal authority—and at least in its analysis, it may have turned *Humphrey's Executor* into a near cipher. It recognized just "two exceptions—one for multimember expert agencies that do not wield substantial executive power, and one for inferior officers with limited duties and no policymaking or administrative authority."[37] In the court's account, these exceptions "'represent what up to now have been the outermost constitutional limits of permissible congressional restrictions on the President's removal power.'"[38]

Let us pause over those sentences. For present purposes, the key exception is for "multimember expert agencies that do not wield substantial executive power." That phrase encompasses a truly minimalist understanding of *Humphrey's Executor*—one that was, to be sure, consistent with the understanding at the time. In *Humphrey's Executor*, the FTC was taken by the court to have "quasi-judicial" authority in the specific sense that it could find facts, which would then be presented to courts in an enforcement proceeding. As the Supreme Court understood matters in 1935, the FTC was acting a lot like a special master.[39] Unlike a court, it did not have the authority, after an adjudication, to issue orders whose violation would result in sanctions. In addition, the FTC was required by law to make reports and recommendations to Congress, and in that specific sense, it was taken by the court as a "quasi-legislative" body.[40] The FTC was not understood, in 1935, to have rulemaking authority.[41] In that sense, *Humphrey's Executor* was, in its time, a narrow holding. As the court then saw it, the FTC had exceedingly limited powers and was not in any sense exercising executive authority.[42]

In the coming decades, *Humphrey's Executor* came to be understood far more broadly.[43] It was widely taken to validate modern independent agencies, which make rules and engage in multiple (other) executive functions.[44] In these circumstances, *Seila Law* can be seen as a thunderclap. Many independent agencies, including the SEC, the FCC, the Nuclear Regulatory Commission, and the National Labor Relations Board, "wield substantial executive power," if only because they promulgate regulations. Do they fall outside the "exception" recognized in *Humphrey's Executor*? That would be a radical conclusion, consistent with the Grand Narrative—and *Seila Law* leaves it open. In 2025, the Trump administration rejected the idea of independent agencies and is pressing the Supreme Court to overrule *Humphrey's Executor* entirely. If and when the court does that—and there is a good chance that it will—a significant part of the Grand Narrative will be entrenched in law.

"TO SAY WHAT THE LAW IS"

Insofar as it involves Article III, the Grand Narrative has several locations. One involves the allocation of interpretive authority between courts and agencies. In *Chevron v. NRDC*,[45] the court famously ruled that if Congress has not spoken clearly or directly, then judges should uphold agency interpretations of law, so long as those interpretations are reasonable. *Chevron* was characterized by some as "a counter-*Marbury* revolution, one at war with the APA [Administrative Procedure Act], time honored precedents, and so much surrounding law."[46] In rejecting *Chevron*, *Loper Bright* relied on section 706 of the APA, which states in relevant part that "court must decide all relevant questions of law."[47] At the same time, the court spoke grandly. It repeatedly drew attention to Article III and *Marbury v. Madison*:

> The Framers also envisioned that the final "interpretation of the laws" would be "the proper and peculiar province of the courts." Unlike the political branches, the courts would by design exercise "neither Force nor Will, but merely judgment." To ensure the "steady, upright and impartial administration of the laws," the Framers structured the Constitution to allow judges to exercise that judgment independent of influence from the political branches. This Court embraced the Framers' understanding of the judicial function early on. In the foundational decision of *Marbury v. Madison*, Chief Justice Marshall famously declared that "[i]t is emphatically the province and duty of the judicial department to say what the law is."[48]

In its return to constitutional fundamentals, *Loper Bright* sounds a lot like *Seila Law*. The court added: "The APA thus codifies for agency cases the unremarkable, yet elemental proposition reflected by judicial practice dating back to Marbury: that courts decide legal questions by applying their own judgment."[49] It is easy to see *Loper Bright* as reflecting the Grand Narrative insofar as it can be taken to assert, and reclaim, judicial authority in the interpretation of federal law.

"PUBLIC RIGHTS" CABINED

What about *Crowell*? That decision had several components. In private rights cases, the court held, administrative tribunals could find facts subject to deferential review, except for jurisdictional and constitutional facts, where de novo review was required.[50] *Crowell* added that administrative tribunals could find facts in "public rights" cases without review by Article III courts. The *Crowell* court defined private rights cases as those involving "the liability of one individual to another under the law as defined."[51] The court also said that a matter of public right is one "between the government and persons subject to its authority in connection with the performance of the constitutional functions of the executive or legislative departments."[52]

That statement launched an ornate body of law, raising the question whether a public right case might be found whenever the government was a party (thus simplifying a number of Article III problems), or whether a public right might exist when the relevant right was created by Congress. The cases on this point were exceedingly complicated, and there have been many fluctuations.[53]

In *Jarkesy*, however, the court, evidently motivated by the Grand Narrative, dramatically narrowed the public rights exception. It pointed to "historic categories of adjudications" that "fall within the exception, including relations with Indian tribes, the administration of public lands, and the granting of public benefits such as payments to veterans, pensions, and patent rights."[54] That is a list, not a theory. Whatever happened to the old idea that a matter of public right is one "between the government and persons subject to its authority in connection with the performance of the constitutional functions of the executive or legislative departments"?

The basic point is that with the Grand Narrative in mind, the *Jarkesy* court was plainly uncomfortable with a long train of decisions involving both Article III and the Seventh Amendment. It fundamentally recast, and narrowed, the public rights exception. It did not overrule *Crowell*, to be sure, or even question it (at least not explicitly), but Justice Gorsuch made his own views plain, writing, "To get there [in *Crowell*] took a dash of fiction and a pinch of surmise."[55] Thus "the Court embraced the fiction that Executive Branch officials might similarly act as assistants or adjuncts to Article III courts. . . . Almost in a blink . . . more and more agencies began assuming adjudicatory functions previously reserved for judges and juries, employing novel procedures that sometimes bore faint resemblance to those observed in court."[56] A clearer statement of the Grand Narrative would be hard to find. There might be a whirlwind to reap.

LAWMAKING
In *Gundy v. United States*,[57] the court was asked to use the nondelegation doctrine to strike down a grant of discretion to the attorney general. The court declined the invitation, construing the relevant statute so as to avoid the nondelegation problem.[58] In dissent, Justice Gorsuch, joined by Chief Justice Roberts and Justice Thomas, offered a large-scale attack not only on the majority's analysis, but also on the decades of law since *Schechter Poultry*.[59] Here is a flavor:

If Congress could pass off its legislative power to the executive branch, the "[v]est-
ing [c]lauses, and indeed the entire structure of the Constitution," would "make
no sense." Without the involvement of representatives from across the country or
the demands of bicameralism and presentment, legislation would risk becoming
nothing more than the will of the current President. And if laws could be simply
declared by a single person, they would not be few in number, the product of
widespread social consensus, likely to protect minority interests, or apt to provide
stability and fair notice. Accountability would suffer too. Legislators might seek to
take credit for addressing a pressing social problem by sending it to the executive
for resolution, while at the same time blaming the executive for the problems that
attend whatever measures he chooses to pursue.[60]

Invoking what he saw as the plain meaning of Article I, section 1, Justice
Gorsuch urged that the "intelligible principle" test had become no test at
all and that the court should abandon it or discipline it with a new and
stricter test.[61] Justice Alito did not join Justice Gorsuch, but he expressed
clear dissatisfaction with the state of the law: "Nevertheless, since 1935,
the Court has uniformly rejected nondelegation arguments and has upheld
provisions that authorized agencies to adopt important rules pursuant to
extraordinarily capacious standards. If a majority of this Court were willing
to reconsider the approach we have taken for the past 84 years, I would
support that effort."[62] It is worth pausing over those sentences. Justice Alito
clearly expressed dissatisfaction *with an approach taken for 84 years*. He was
speaking favorably of a central aspect of the Grand Narrative.

Turn in this light to the *major questions doctrine*, as the court calls it,
which holds that agencies may not make certain "extraordinary decisions"
without clear congressional authorization.[63] I will have more to say about
the major questions doctrine in chapter 10, but for the moment, notice
that it is impossible to understand that doctrine without reference to the
Grand Narrative.

As the court has explained it, the major questions doctrine has clear
roots in the separation of powers and more specifically the nondelegation
doctrine. The basic idea is that certain decisions, large or transformative,
require unambiguous congressional authorization. Agencies cannot make
such decisions without that authorization. As the court put it in *West Virginia v. EPA*, "In certain extraordinary cases, both separation of powers principles and a practical understanding of legislative intent make us 'reluctant
to read into ambiguous statutory text' the delegation claimed to be lurking
there. To convince us otherwise, something more than a merely plausible

textual basis for the agency action is necessary. The agency instead must point to 'clear congressional authorization' for the power it claims."[64] Let us underline the term *separation of powers* in that passage, which points to the Grand Narrative.

Justice Gorsuch is particularly taken with the Grand Narrative, and in his view, the major questions doctrine has everything to do with the non-delegation doctrine.[65] According to Justice Gorsuch, the doctrine is a clear-statement principle, akin to the presumption against retroactivity and the presumption against abrogation of sovereign immunity. Clearly invoking the Grand Narrative, Justice Gorsuch urges that "Article I's Vesting Clause has its own [clear-statement principle]: the major questions doctrine."[66] As he puts it, "The Court has applied the major questions doctrine for the same reason it has applied other similar clear-statement rules—to ensure that the government does 'not inadvertently cross constitutional lines.'"[67]

The goal of the doctrine is thus to ensure congressional primacy by avoiding a situation in which agencies exercise authority that the national legislature has not clearly granted them. On this view, the major questions doctrine is best understood as a nondelegation canon, akin to the presumption against retroactivity. Because Article I is central to the doctrine, we are clearly seeing the Grand Narrative in action.

COUNTERNARRATIVES

The Grand Narrative is immensely powerful. One reason is its simplicity: It is easy to grasp. You can get it instantly. Another is its narrative resonance: It is a familiar tale of a rise (the founding),[68] a fall (the New Deal),[69] and a possible redemption.[70] It has energy and a charge. It sits on a high horse.

To its defenders, it has firm roots in the Constitution itself. It is what the separation of powers is about. Anyone who reads the document will not like the idea of a headless fourth branch of government—or of lawmaking by the executive branch, execution by people immunized from presidential control, or adjudication by people lacking the safeguards of Article III. The idea of a headless fourth branch is blunt, direct, and memorable. Indeed, the Grand Narrative is not only animating those aspects of administrative law; it also helps to explain the recent intensification of judicial review of agency action in many domains—including, above all, arbitrariness review.[71]

Many defenders of the Grand Narrative are originalists. They believe that the meaning of the Constitution is settled by its original public meaning. They think that the original public meaning of Articles I, II, and III fit well with, and call for, the Grand Narrative. Whether this is so depends, of course, on what the original public meaning turns out to be. But there is a great deal of historical work purporting to show that the original public meaning does, in fact, support the Grand Narrative.

I should say that I have some admiration for the Grand Narrative because it puts liberty and deliberative democracy front and center. Those who believe in it should be regarded with respect. They are defenders of freedom.

But none of this is meant to suggest that the Grand Narrative is correct. For some people, it is snake oil; in my view, it overreads what the separation of power entails.[72] It might be snake oil because it is wrong on its own premises; it might be snake oil because its premises are wrong. We can imagine four kinds of rebuttals, and each can produce a narrative of its own (if perhaps not quite so grand). Note here that the Grand Narrative consists of *three* grand narratives, and each must be taken on its own terms. It would be possible, for example, to think that the Grand Narrative is correct with respect to Article III, but that it is false with respect to Article I and Article II. Let's now turn to the four rebuttals. Of these, the second and the fourth are my favorites.

ORIGINALISM

I have said that the rise of the Grand Narrative is closely associated with the rise of originalism in constitutional law, and hence it is natural and appropriate to evaluate it in originalist terms. Does it in fact fit the original public meaning?[73] To answer that question, the Grand Narrative must be assessed carefully, both in historical terms and area by area. Some parts of the Grand Narrative are more plausible than others, and I restrict myself to a few brief notes here. Mounting historical work suggests that from the originalist standpoint,[74] the idea of a nondelegation doctrine, understood as a ban on the grant of open-ended discretionary power, may well be a myth[75]— perhaps even a concoction of the twentieth century.[76] In other words, the mounting work raises the possibility that the nondelegation doctrine, so understood, is inconsistent with the original public meaning of the founding document. If so, we are speaking of something like an invented tradition[77] or the construction of memory.[78]

A great deal of evidence shows that the founding generation simply did not believe that the Constitution limited Congress's power to grant broad discretion to others, above all the executive branch.[79] The evidence takes the form of a demonstration that the founding generation was broadly comfortable with such open-ended grants. If so, the original public meaning of Article I, section 1 may not support the nondelegation doctrine as Justice Gorsuch (for example) understands it. According to a more cautious view, the founding generation was comfortable with broad grants of discretion, and the original public meaning did not forbid them. But still, we cannot say that an entirely open-ended grant would have been deemed permissible.

Suppose, for example, that Congress said this: "The president may issue any regulations that he shall deem proper to handle the problem of climate change." Nothing in the relevant history permits a law of that kind. In other words, the existence of some nondelegation doctrine, banning that kind of wildly open-ended grant, is not ruled out, but the Grand Narrative gets the original public meaning wrong insofar as it suggests that Article I, section 1 forbids Congress from giving agencies the kinds of discretion that they currently enjoy.[80] In my view, the more cautious view is essentially correct.

In addition, there is some compelling historical evidence that from the originalist standpoint,[81] the argument in favor of unrestricted presidential removal power may also be a myth—perhaps another concoction of the twentieth century, not the eighteenth. Within the founding generation, many people believed that Congress could limit the president's removal power over high-level employees, including (some) principal officers.[82] For some, and contrary to the Grand Narrative, the Decision of 1789 is mysterious, not straightforward. If we count the votes, what happened in 1789 seems to undermine the Grand Narrative, rather than support it, though the evidence is not entirely clear.[83]

With respect to Article III, we can find considerable historical support for the view that Congress may grant at least some adjudicatory functions to agencies.[84] *Crowell* itself might turn out to be defensible on originalist grounds. At the same time, *Jarkesy* might well have gotten the public rights exception, well, right, because the court seems to have captured longstanding practice with respect to the permissible categories of exclusion from federal courts.

Final conclusions would require extended analysis, but it might well follow that some (not all) of the Grand Narrative should be seen as a form of living constitutionalism, dressed up in founding era garb that really does not fit. The originalist counternarrative, based on some meticulous historical work, sees important parts of the Grand Narrative as an invention. Of course, a great deal more would have to be said to evaluate that conclusion.

BURKEANISM

Should we be originalists? That is a disputed question. In my view, we should not be.[85] If we are not originalists, then we might be Burkeans, understanding the Constitution in line not with the original meaning, but with long-standing traditions. If we do not credit the founding-era evidence against the Grand Narrative, we might nonetheless reject it on Burkean grounds.[86]

Burke's key claim is that the "science of constructing a commonwealth, or reforming it, is, like every other experimental science, not to be taught a priori."[87] To make this argument, Burke opposes theories and abstractions—developed by individual minds—to traditions, built up by many minds over long periods. In a particularly vivid passage, Burke writes:

> We wished at the period of the Revolution, and do now wish, to derive all we possess as *an inheritance from our forefathers*. . . . The science of government being therefore so practical in itself, and intended for such practical purposes, a matter which requires experience, and even more experience than any person can gain in his whole life, however sagacious and observing he may be, it is with infinite caution than any man ought to venture upon pulling down an edifice which has answered in any tolerable degree, for ages the common purposes of society, or on building it up again, without having models and patterns of approved utility before his eyes.[88]

In the context of constitutional law, including the separation of powers, contemporary Burkeans urge that judges should interpret ambiguous constitutional provisions by close reference to long-standing practices. Recall Justice Alito's words: "If a majority of this Court were willing to reconsider the approach we have taken for the past 84 years, I would support that effort."[89] A committed Burkean would not like that at all.

If we are faithful Burkeans, we would think it exceedingly important that for many decades, agencies have been allowed to exercise broad discretionary power; that independent agencies have been allowed to exist; and that agencies have been permitted to exercise adjudicatory power, subject to a host of constraints. Rejection of the Grand Narrative, for better or for worse, has been woven into the fabric of American institutions. Accepting that narrative, decades into the twenty-first century, would be a kind of hubris—an overhaul of established institutions by those in the grip of a theory. That would be arrogant and wrong. The Burkean counternarrative sees the Grand Narrative as a kind of French Revolution.

THAYERISM

In the late nineteenth century, James Bradley Thayer argued in favor of a sharply limited role for courts in a democratic society.[90] He urged that in the face of a constitutional challenge, all reasonable doubts should be resolved favorably to Congress, in the sense that the Constitution should be interpreted in a way that gives the political process maximum room to maneuver. In a crucial passage, Thayer said that "such questions require an allowance to be made by the judges for the vast and not definable range of legislative power and choice, for that wide margin of considerations which address themselves only to the practical judgment of a legislative body. Within that margin, as among all these legislative considerations, the con-stitutional law-makers must be allowed a free foot."[91]

Under the right approach, "an Act of the legislature is not to be declared void unless the violation of the constitution is so manifest *as to leave no room for reasonable doubt*."[92] Thayer urged that this idea was established "very early" and in fact became entrenched by 1811.[93] What was necessary, for invalidation, was "a clear and unequivocal breach of the Constitution, not a doubtful and argumentative implication."[94] As Thayer put it, courts "can only disregard the Act when those who have the right to make laws have not merely made a mistake, but have made a very clear one,—so clear that it is not open to rational question."[95]

With these words in mind, Thayerians would reject the Grand Narra-tive on the ground that it neglects the fact that the answers it gives are hardly "not open to rational question." In the face of "reasonable doubt," courts should step aside. The Thayerian counternarrative, celebrating judi-cial respect for congressional choices, sees the Grand Narrative as fatally undemocratic.

PRAGMATISM

Suppose we believe that the best approach to the US Constitution under-stands the document as something that should endure over time and that should have the flexibility to accommodate new circumstances and exigencies.[96] On that view, Congress ought to be given some room to adopt institutional arrangements, consistent with the broad commitment to separation of powers, that are, in its view, necessary or appropriate.[97] Those who believe in a pragmatic approach to constitutional interpretation need not be Burkeans; the fact that an innovation is new, rather than old, is not determinative. Nor need they be thoroughgoing Thayerians. They would simply emphasize that the Constitution has to be workable and that so long as we do not have plain defiance of constitutional restrictions, courts ought not to stand in the way.[98]

The questions remain, of course, whether broad grants of discretion are a defiance of Article I; whether the independent agency form is a defiance of Article II; and whether administrative adjudication is a defiance of Article III. Pragmatists would be inclined to say "no" to all these questions. Their own counternarrative, protective of both the separation of powers and the institutional initiatives that have produced the modern administrative state, sees the Grand Narrative as reckless and clueless. They think that it is built on sand.

FOUNDATIONS

It is not possible to understand contemporary administrative law without reference to the Grand Narrative. The foundations of long-standing law have been shaken. *Chevron* is overruled. Rooted in an understanding of the separation of powers, the major questions doctrine holds that in important cases, ambiguous statutes must be interpreted to cabin agency authority. The nondelegation doctrine is no longer a dead letter. *Seila Law* can be taken to say, "go forth and sin no more," or instead to threaten the independent agency form more broadly; as of this writing, the latter seems more likely. The public rights exception has been radically narrowed.

True, we cannot yet say that *Humphrey's Executor, Crowell v. Benson,* and *American Trucking* have been overruled. But we can say that both *Humphrey's Executor* and *Crowell* have been sharply limited, and no one should be amazed if the nondelegation doctrine is used, in the near future, to invalidate federal legislation.

There are strong reasons to question the Grand Narrative. Its roots in the original public meaning are insecure. Some alternative narratives, or counternarratives, are better. If the Grand Narrative continues to be invoked to uproot the fabric of the modern administrative state, it will inaugurate something like a legal revolution, reflecting what (in my view) would have to be called a form of judicial hubris. But for the moment, let us step back a bit. Those who believe in the Grand Narrative are committed to the separation of powers: good for them. If others, also committed to the separation of powers, favor different narratives, then the relevant disputes are between not enemies but friends.

9 NONDELEGATION CANONS

Now let's get a bit technical. We are going to see how the separation of powers is supported in court, almost on a daily basis.

Although federal courts do not vindicate a general nondelegation doctrine, they do enforce a series of more specific and smaller nondelegation doctrines. Rather than invalidating federal legislation as excessively vague and open-ended, courts say that executive agencies may not engage in certain controversial activities unless and until Congress has expressly authorized them to do so. When fundamental rights and interests are at stake, the choices must be made legislatively. As a technical matter, the key holdings are based not on the nondelegation doctrine but on certain "canons" of construction.

What I mean to identify here are the *nondelegation canons*—usually not organized or recognized as such, but central to the operation of modern public law, and designed to ensure clear legislative authorization for certain decisions. These are nondelegation canons for the simple reason that they forbid the executive branch, including administrative agencies, from making decisions on its own. The nondelegation canons are central to the separation of powers. In important respects, they are where it lives and breathes.

Although my emphasis will be on nondelegation canons in American law, the basic idea has analogues in numerous legal systems and indeed plays an important role in many social orders. In the United Kingdom, consider the Human Rights Act of 1998, which governs interpretation of statutes that may conflict with the European Convention on Human Rights. Section 3 declares: "So far as it is possible to do so, primary legislation and subordinate legislation must be read and given effect in a way which is compatible with the Convention rights." In this sense, the Human Rights Act creates a kind of nondelegation canon, requiring express legislative deliberation on behalf of any abridgement of convention rights.

Consider a few examples from the United States. The most important is that executive agencies are not permitted to construe federal statutes in such a way as to raise serious constitutional questions. If the constitutional question is substantial, then Congress must clearly assert its desire to venture into the disputed terrain.[1] This principle means that without clear congressional permission, courts will not permit the executive to intrude on liberty or equality in a way that might compromise the Constitution. Here is a clear effort to link institutional protections with individual rights: It can be difficult to get specific language through Congress, and hence a requirement of congressional specificity helps protect rights by ensuring that any interference with them must be clearly authorized and supported by both Congress and the executive.

In addition, Congress must affirmatively and specifically authorize the extraterritorial application of federal law. Agencies cannot exercise their discretion, under an ambiguous statutory provision, so as to apply national law outside of American borders. A clear congressional statement to this effect is required. So too: When treaties and statutes are ambiguous, they must be construed favorably to Native American tribes. The agency's own judgment, if it is an exercise of discretion, is irrelevant.[2]

One of my central purposes here is to show that these canons should be understood as entirely legitimate and that they should be used even more than they now are. The nondelegation canons represent a salutary kind of *democracy-forcing judicial minimalism*, designed to ensure that certain choices are made by an institution with a superior democratic pedigree. Indeed, the nondelegation canons turn out to be a contemporary incarnation of the founding effort to link protection of individual rights, and other important interests, with separation of powers. In certain cases, Congress must decide the key questions on its own. This is the enduring function of the nondelegation doctrine, and it is endorsed, not repudiated, by current law.

NONDELEGATION CANONS, 1: CONSTITUTIONAL INSPIRATION

Some nondelegation canons have constitutional origins. They are often designed to promote some goal, often involving rights, with a constitutional foundation.

Consider, as the most familiar example, the idea that executive agencies will not be permitted to construe statutes in such a way as to raise serious constitutional doubts.[3] Notice that this principle goes well beyond the (uncontroversial) notion that agencies should not be allowed to construe statutes so as to be unconstitutional. The principle is much broader than that: Constitutionally sensitive questions will not be permitted to arise unless the constitutionally designated lawmaker has deliberately and expressly chosen to raise them. For example, a law will not ordinarily be taken to allow the executive branch to intrude on the right to travel, violate the right to free speech, interfere with religious liberty, or constitute a taking of private property without compensation. If Congress seeks to raise a serious constitutional question, it must do so explicitly.

The only limitations on the principle are that the constitutional doubts must be substantial and that the statute must be fairly susceptible to an interpretation that does not raise those doubts.[4] So long as the statute is unclear and the constitutional question serious, Congress must decide to raise that question via express statement.

Belonging in the same category is the idea that the executive agencies will not be allowed to interpret ambiguous provisions so as to preempt state law.[5] The constitutional source of this principle is the constitutional commitment to a federal structure. That commitment may not be compromised without a clear congressional decision to do so—an important requirement in light of the various safeguards against cavalier disregard of state interests created by the system of state representation in Congress.[6] Notice that most of the time, there is no constitutional barrier to national preemption; Congress is usually entitled to preempt state law if it chooses. But there is a constitutional obstacle of a sort: the preemption decision must be made legislatively, not by the executive.[7]

As a third example, consider the notion that unless Congress has spoken with clarity, agencies are not allowed to apply statutes retroactively.[8] Because retroactivity is disfavored in the law,[9] Congress will not be taken to have delegated to the executive branch the authority to decide the question. The best way to understand this idea is as an institutional echo of the notion that the Due Process Clause forbids retroactive application of law.[10] The constitutional constraints on retroactivity are now modest; though the Ex Post Facto Clause in the American Constitution forbids retroactive application of the criminal law, the clause is narrowly construed, and Congress is generally permitted to impose civil legislation retroactively if it chooses.[11]

But there is an institutional requirement here. Congress must make that choice explicitly and take the political heat for deciding to do so. It will not be taken to have attempted the same result via delegation, and the executive branch will not be taken to have the authority to choose retroactivity on its own. Perhaps part of the courts' motivation here is ambivalence about judicial refusal to apply the Ex Post Facto Clause or the Due Process Clause so as to call into constitutional question some retroactive applications of civil law. The nondelegation canon is a more cautious way of promoting the relevant concerns.

Consider, finally, the extremely important *rule of lenity*, which says that in the face of ambiguity, criminal statutes will be construed favorably to criminal defendants. One function of the lenity principle is to ensure against delegations, to courts or to anyone else. Criminal law must be a product of a clear judgment on Congress's part. Where Congress has made no such judgment, the statute will not apply merely because it is plausibly interpreted, by courts or enforcement authorities, to fit the case at hand. The rule of lenity is inspired by the due process constraint on convicting people of crimes under open-ended or vague statutes. Although it is not itself a constitutional mandate, the rule is rooted in a constitutional principle and serves as a time-honored nondelegation canon.

NONDELEGATION CANONS, 2: SOVEREIGNTY

The second category of nondelegation canons contains principles that have a foundation in widespread understandings about the nature of governmental authority—more particularly, in widespread understandings about sovereignty. Consider here the fact that the executive is not permitted to apply statutes outside of the territorial borders of the United States.[12] If statutes are to receive extraterritorial application, it must be as a result of a deliberate congressional judgment to this effect. The central idea here is that extraterritorial application calls for extremely sensitive judgments involving international relations; such judgments must be made via the ordinary lawmaking process (in which the president, of course, participates). The executive may not make this decision on its own.[13] One of the evident purposes of this requirement is now familiar: to ensure deliberation among diverse people, and not merely within the executive branch, before American law will be applied abroad.

For broadly related reasons, the executive branch cannot interpret statutes and treaties unfavorably to Native Americans.[14] Where statutory provisions are ambiguous, the government will not prevail. This idea is plainly an outgrowth of the complex history of relations between the United States and Native American tribes, which have semisovereign status; it is an effort to ensure that any unfavorable outcome will be a product of an explicit judgment from the national legislature. The institutional checks created by congressional structure must be navigated before an adverse decision may be made.

Consider, as a final illustration, the fact that the executive branch is not permitted to waive the sovereign immunity of the United States, and indeed statutory ambiguity cannot be used by that branch as a basis for a waiver, which must be explicit in legislation.[15] Sovereign immunity is a background structural understanding, defeasible only on the basis of a judgment to that effect by the national legislature.

NONDELEGATION CANONS, 3: LEGISLATIVE SUPREMACY

The final set of nondelegation canons is designed to recognize legislative supremacy in certain domains. For example, exemptions from taxation are narrowly construed;[16] the executive cannot exempt people on its own. If it wants to exempt a group from federal income tax, then it must find clear authorization from Congress. A central idea here may be that such exemptions are often the product of lobbying efforts by well-organized private groups and thus a reflection of factional influence; the executive may not create such exemptions on its own.

At the same time, there is a general federal policy against anticompetitive practices, and the executive will not be permitted to seize on ambiguous statutory language so as to defeat that policy.[17] If Congress wants to make an exception to the policy in favor of competition, it is certainly permitted to do so. But the executive may not do so without congressional instruction. So, too, it is presumed that statutes providing veterans' benefits will be construed generously to veterans, and the executive cannot conclude otherwise.[18] This idea is an analogue to the notion that statutes will be construed favorably to Native Americans; both require a congressional judgment if a group perceived as weak or deserving is going to be treated harshly.

In decisions of particular importance for the modern regulatory state, agencies are sometimes forbidden to require very large expenditures for trivial or de minimis gains.[19] If Congress wants to be "absolutist" about safety, in a way that might well compromise social well-being, it is permitted to do so by explicit statement, but the executive will not be allowed to take ambiguous language in this direction. This is a genuinely novel nondelegation principle, a creation of the late twentieth century. It is an evident response to perceived problems in modern regulatory policy.

INSTITUTIONS AND RIGHTS

Canons of the sort I have outlined here are not uncontroversial. Judge Richard Posner, for example, fears that some of them create a "penumbral Constitution," authorizing judges to bend statutes in particular directions even though there may in fact be no constitutional violation.[20] But if the analysis here is correct, then there is a simple answer to these concerns: The relevant canons operate as nondelegation principles, rooted in the separation of powers. They are designed to ensure that Congress decides certain contested questions on its own. If this idea is a core structural commitment of the Constitution, and if it ensures congresssional deliberation on sensitive issues, then there can be no problem with its judicial enforcement.

I have suggested that there are serious problems with judicial enforcement of the conventional nondelegation doctrine. Compare, along the relevant dimensions, judicial use of the nondelegation canons. Here the institutional problem is far less severe. Courts do not ask the hard-to-manage question whether the legislature has exceeded the permissible level of discretion, but pose instead the far more manageable question whether the executive has clearly been given the discretion to decide something that (under the appropriate canon) only legislatures may decide. In other words, courts ask a question about subject matter, not a question about degree.

Putting the competence of courts to one side, the nondelegation canons have the salutary function of ensuring that certain important rights and interests will not be compromised unless Congress has expressly decided to compromise them. Thus, the nondelegation canons lack a central defect of the conventional doctrine: Although there is no good reason to think that a reinvigorated nondelegation doctrine would improve the operation of modern government, it is entirely reasonable to think that for certain kinds of decisions, merely executive decisions are not enough.

If, for example, an agency is attempting on its own to apply domestic law extraterritorially, then we might believe that whatever its expertise, it is inappropriate, as a matter of democratic theory and international relations, for this to happen unless Congress has decided that it should. Or courts might reasonably believe that retroactive application of regulatory law is acceptable not simply because the executive believes that an ambiguous law should be so construed, but if and only if Congress has reached this conclusion. This judgment might be founded on the idea that political safeguards will ensure that Congress will so decide only if there is very good reason for that decision. For those who believe that retroactivity is constitutionally unacceptable, this may be insufficient consolation. But a requirement that Congress make the decision on its own is certainly likely to make abuses less common, if they are legitimately characterized as abuses at all.

These points have the considerable advantage of understanding the nondelegation canons as a modern incarnation of the framers' basic project of linking individual rights and institutional design. The link comes from protecting certain rights and interests not through a flat judicial ban on governmental action, but through a requirement that certain controversial or unusual actions will occur only with respect for the institutional safeguards introduced through the design of Congress. There is thus a close connection between the nondelegation canons and a central aspiration of the constitutional structure.

The most important future debates will involve not the existence or legitimacy of nondelegation canons, but their particular content. Of course, the category changes over time. A core nondelegation canon of the early twentieth century required a clear legislative statement to authorize an interference with common law rights. For the most part, this canon is no longer reflected in current law. By contrast, the idea that statutes will be construed so as to require de minimis exceptions is relatively new, a creation of the late twentieth century and a self-conscious judicial response to certain problems in regulatory law. It would be easy to imagine the introduction of new canons (as we will see in the next chapter) and the repudiation of current ones. I have attempted to sketch defenses of existing nondelegation canons in order to understand the basis for the view that the relevant issues may not be resolved by the executive alone. But nothing in the general account depends on whether any particular canons are defensible.

As a class, the nondelegation canons are best defended on the ground that certain decisions are ordinarily expected to be made by the national legislature, with its various institutional safeguards, and not via the executive. A central goal of those safeguards is to ensure against the problems that occur when like-minded people are deliberating with one another and failing to confront alternative views. In this way, the nondelegation canons take their place as one of the most prominent domains in which protection of individual rights, and of other important interests, occurs not through blanket prohibitions on governmental action but through channeling decisions to particular governmental institutions—in this case, Congress itself.

10 THE MAJOR QUESTIONS DOCTRINE

The newest nondelegation canon, and currently one of the most important, goes by the name of the *major questions doctrine*. Under the major questions doctrine, which we briefly encountered earlier, executive agencies are not allowed to act in ways that have extraordinary[1] or staggering[2] "economic and political significance"[3] unless Congress has clearly authorized them to do so. What underlies this idea? There are two possible answers.[4]

The first, most clearly developed by Justice Neil Gorsuch, is simple: the separation of powers.[5] The basic idea is inspired by a particular understanding of John Locke, who wrote: "The legislative cannot transfer the power of making laws to any other hands, for it being but a delegated power from the people, they who have it cannot pass it over to others. . . . And when the people have said, 'We will submit, and be governed by laws made by such men, and in such forms,' nobody else can say other men shall make laws for them; nor can they be bound by any laws but such as are enacted by those whom they have chosen and authorized to make laws for them."[6]

In Justice Gorsuch's view, the major questions doctrine "operates to protect foundational constitutional guarantees."[7] According to Justice Gorsuch, the doctrine is a nondelegation canon, akin to the presumption against retroactivity and the presumption against abrogation of sovereign immunity. The goal of the doctrine is thus to ensure congressional primacy by avoiding a situation in which agencies exercise authority that the national legislature has not clearly granted them..[8] Its apparently recent creation is a serious challenge for the view that it is a product of Article I's Vesting Clause, but efforts have been made to suggest that it is not as novel and freewheeling as it appears.[9]

Justice Amy Coney Barrett rejects this view and offers a different and more low-key defense of the major questions doctrine.[10] In her account, it has little or nothing to do with the separation of powers, at least in the first instance. Instead, it has everything to do with how communication ordinarily works. To see what she has in mind, consider this footnote from Wittgenstein: "Someone says to me: 'Shew the children a game.' I teach them gaming with dice, and the other says 'I didn't mean that sort of game.' Must the exclusion of the game with dice have come before his mind when he gave me the order?"[11]

The answer to Wittgenstein's question is "no." If someone asks me to show a "game" to children, gambling is ordinarily not included in the category of *game*, even though it is technically a game. The same is true of Russian roulette, spin the bottle, and boxing. We can understand Wittgenstein to be using a form of the major questions doctrine, applied to ordinary conversation. If someone asks me to show the children a game, to go get lunch at the grocery store (rat poison?), or to make a restaurant reservation for Wednesday night (the most expensive place in town?), "extraordinary" or "staggering" choices, on my part, require strong contextual justification. "I didn't mean that sort of lunch" or "I didn't mean that sort of restaurant": In ordinary conversation, people anticipate that response, and they do not make choices that would elicit it.

Whether or not she was aware of it, Justice Barrett's motivating example is exceedingly close to Wittgenstein's. It involves "a parent who hires a babysitter to watch her young children over the weekend."[12] The parent tells the babysitter the following: "Make sure the kids have fun." Suppose that the babysitter takes the children on an overnight adventure, complete with roller coaster rides. Justice Barrett can be taken to urge, sensibly enough, that the parent might think something like: "I didn't mean that sort of fun."[13] Justice Barrett writes: "In the normal course, permission to spend money on fun authorizes a babysitter to take children to the local ice cream parlor or movie theater, not on a multiday excursion to an out-of-town amusement park. If a parent were willing to greenlight a trip that big, we would expect much more clarity than a general instruction to 'make sure the kids have fun.'"[14]

Justice Barrett is keenly aware, of course, that context matters. We might learn that the parent left out suitcases or that history shows that the babysitter is authorized to take the kids on such an outing. In Justice Barrett's view, the major questions doctrine operates in the same way: "Just as we would expect a parent to give more than a general instruction if she intended to authorize a babysitter-led getaway, we also 'expect Congress to speak clearly if it wishes to assign to an agency decisions of vast "economic and political significance."'"[15]

Thus far, then, we are speaking of ordinary principles of communication; there is no need to invoke the Constitution or the separation of powers. Nonetheless, and notably, Justice Barrett fortifies her approach by reference to "the basic premise that Congress normally 'intends to make major policy decisions itself, not leave those decisions to agencies.'"[16] In light of Article I, section 1, "a reasonable interpreter would expect [Congress] to make the big-time policy calls itself, rather than pawning them off to another branch."[17]

Nonetheless, Justice Barrett's approach is meaningfully different from Justice Gorsuch's. In her view, the major questions doctrine is emphatically *not* a clear-statement rule. It is not "a normative rule that *discourages* Congress from empowering agencies."[18] It imposes no "clarity tax" on Congress.[19] Far from it. Under her approach (and unlike under Gorsuch's), courts do not have permission "to choose an inferior-but-tenable alternative that curbs the agency's authority—and that marks a key difference between [her] view and the 'clear statement' view of the major questions doctrine."[20] For Justice Barrett, courts must always choose the best interpretation; they do not require a clear statement.

In short: The major questions doctrine is relevant to what the best interpretation is, but if Congress is best understood to have said, "Actually I did mean that sort of game," or perhaps better, "I did not mean that sort of game," or best of all, "I meant the sort of game that the relevant agency deemed to be a game," then the fact that a major question is involved is neither here nor there.

On this view, the major questions doctrine is emphatically not a substantive canon.[21] Justice Barrett is a textualist, and she is cautious about the whole idea of substantive canons.[22] As she explains, such canons, seen as "rules of construction that advance values external to a statute," may operate either as tiebreakers or as far more than that.[23] "Strong-form" canons, including nondelegation canons, require a clear statement.[24] Some strong-form canons have a long pedigree; consider constitutional avoidance and the presumption against retroactivity.[25] Justice Barrett is aware that strong-form canons are "in significant tension with textualism," and she is evidently uncomfortable with them.[26] Speaking directly to arguments like Justice Gorsuch's, she adds, "Even assuming that the federal courts have not overstepped by adopting such canons in the past, I am wary of adopting new ones—and if the major questions doctrine were a newly minted strong-form canon, I would not embrace it."[27]

CHALLENGES AND CONCERNS

Who is right? Both? Neither? It would be possible, of course, to think that Justice Barrett is right about how communication works but also to insist that Justice Gorsuch is right about the need for, and the legitimacy of, a strong-form substantive canon. Justice Barrett has an objection to Justice Gorsuch, but Justice Gorsuch need not have an objection to Justice Barrett, except to the extent that she has an objection to him. Let us begin, in that light, with Justice Barrett.

Her strongest argument points to how communication normally operates. An extraordinary or staggering interpretation of a term might well produce the reaction of "I did not mean that sort of game." Take the use of the word *modify* in the *MCI* case.[28] The governing statute requires common communications carriers to file tariffs with the Federal Communications Commission (FCC), but it also authorizes the Commission to "modify any requirement made by or under . . . this section."[29] The FCC decided to make tariff filing optional for all "nondominant" long-distance carriers.[30] (The only dominant carrier was American Telephone and Telegraph Company.)[31] Much of the court's opinion was textualist.[32] *Modify*, in the court's view, connotes incremental change.[33]

As the court put it: "It might be good English to say that the French Revolution 'modified' the status of the French nobility but only because there is a figure of speech called understatement and a literary device known as sarcasm."[34] Pointing to "the enormous importance to the statutory scheme of the tariff-filing provision,"[35] the court declined to allow the FCC to read *modify* so broadly.[36] In other words: Congress didn't mean *that sort* of "modify."[37] So understood, *MCI* did not create a new clear-statement principle or use heavy constitutional artillery to constrain the FCC's discretion. It was simply applying Wittgenstein's point about how communication works.

An analysis of this sort could plausibly make sense of other major questions cases.[38] Note as well that if the major questions doctrine is understood in this way, it is not only an obstacle to what might be seen as regulatory excess; it is an obstacle to regulatory retrenchment or deregulation as well. If a parent tells a babysitter, "have some fun with them," then a babysitter would be violating those instructions if an afternoon involved five minutes of fun and many hours of grueling math exercises. The relevant neutrality of Justice Barrett's approach is a point in its favor; it suggests that she is not wielding the major questions doctrine in what might be seen as a political or ideological manner.[39]

Nonetheless, there is a weakness in Justice Barrett's argument, and it involves (guess what) the separation of powers. It can be found in her reference to "the basic premise that Congress normally 'intends to make major policy decisions itself, not leave those decisions to agencies.'"[40] At first glance, it is not clear that she needs that "premise." We might agree that words are ordinarily understood not to entail staggering or extraordinary conclusions without making judgments about what an abstraction called "Congress" normally intends. But Justice Barrett evidently believed that the premise is helpful or perhaps even necessary. Perhaps it is. If, and to the extent that, Congress intends agencies to make major policy decisions, then Congress *wants* agencies to figure out what sort of game to play, and Justice Barrett's argument runs into serious difficulty.

Is the example of the parent instructing the babysitter really analogous? Is Congress like a parent, and is an agency like a babysitter? Might that example load some dice? More concretely: What is the foundation of the premise that Congress intends to make major policy decisions itself? What kind of "premise" is it? It sounds like an empirical claim.[41] If so, is it true? A great deal depends on the meaning of the words *normally* and *major*. But there is a good argument that the premise is not correct—or at least that it is overstated and misleading.

To put it bluntly, Congress often (whether *normally* or not) *does* intend to leave major policy decisions to the executive. Certainly this is so if we consider the text of the statutory terms. Consider, for example, a key provision of the Clean Air Act,[42] which instructs the Environmental Protection Agency (EPA) to set standards, "the attainment and maintenance of which . . . are requisite to protect the public health" with "an adequate margin of safety."[43]

Or consider the National Traffic and Motor Vehicle Safety Act of 1966,[44] which directs the secretary of transportation to issue motor vehicle safety standards that "shall be practicable, meet the need for motor vehicle safety, and be stated in objective terms."[45] Or consider this important statute:

> Not later than 12 months after the date of the enactment of this Act, the Secretary shall initiate a rulemaking to revise Federal Motor Vehicle Safety Standard 111 (FMVSS 111) to expand the required field of view to enable the driver of a motor vehicle to detect areas behind the motor vehicle to reduce death and injury resulting from backing incidents, particularly incidents involving small children and disabled persons. The Secretary may prescribe different requirements for different types of motor vehicles to expand the required field of view to enable the driver of a motor vehicle to detect areas behind the motor vehicle to reduce death and injury resulting from backing incidents, particularly incidents involving small children and disabled persons. Such standard may be met by the provision of additional mirrors, sensors, cameras, or other technology to expand the driver's field of view.[46]

What is noteworthy about this statute is that Congress has clearly given the secretary the power to make "major policy choices."[47] The secretary can choose additional mirrors, sensors, cameras, or other technology.[48] Granting that authority *was* Congress's intent.

These are not, of course, atypical examples, from the founding period to the present.[49] Although Congress does often seek to make major policy choices, it also often decides, for one reason or another, not to do that. One reason might be a lack of information about facts; recall chapter 6. (What is the best technology to reduce backing incidents?) Another reason might be a lack of information about how to settle complex policy issues. (With different costs and benefits, how should the government choose among mirrors, sensors, cameras, or other technologies?) Another reason might be the inevitability of changing circumstances. (What if cameras turn out to be much less expensive than anticipated?) Another reason might be a belief that political pressures will lead to bad choices; a more insulated body might do better. (Should Congress specify standards for exposure to silica in the workplace?) Another reason might be a desire not to take political heat. (Should Congress specify the value of a statistical life? Should Congress say that it is $8 million, or $10 million, or $30 million?[50] That is certainly a major policy choice, and Congress has long declined to make it.) Yet another reason might be an inability to achieve consensus. In short, and to invoke Wittgenstein once more, Justice Barrett appears to have been held captive by a picture[51]—a picture about what an abstraction called Congress normally intends.

Perhaps what Justice Barrett describes as the *basic premise* is not an empirical claim at all, but a normative one with respect to the separation of powers. It might be in the nature of a legal fiction, or an article of faith, grounded in Article I, section 1. If it is a legal fiction, then perhaps it is a benign one, or a constitutionally motivated one. If so, it starts to converge with the Lockean argument; it is no longer so Wittgensteinian. It does not involve a linguistic canon anymore; it starts to look like a clear-statement principle. The analogy to the parent and the babysitter tends to fall apart, unless we think that Congress must, as a matter of constitutional principle or at least constitutional "premise," be taken to be the kind of parent who does not delegate a lot of discretion to babysitters. The claim might be that courts rightly assume that Congress does want to make the major policy choices, and the reason is the Constitution itself. Under the founding document, that is, Congress is like a parent who is presumed not to want to give a great deal of discretion, or the power to make very surprising (or major) choices, to a delegate.

At this point, Justice Gorsuch might have two things to say to Justice Barrett. First: She really should not worry so much about the relationship between textualism and substantive canons! Although textualism is fundamentally the right approach, he might continue, it has always been qualified by substantive canons that operate as clear-statement principles.[52] We have seen that the rule of lenity is one example;[53] so is the presumption against extraterritoriality;[54] so is the presumption against retroactivity; so is the Avoidance Canon.[55] Textualism is an approach, not a religion, and it must be defended. Any plausible defense of textualism will not leave substantive canons off-limits. After all, Anglo-American law has long embraced them. For that reason, Justice Gorsuch might accept Justice Barrett's Wittgensteinian argument, but he might add that she should accept his Lockean argument and insist that she actually needs it to make her "premise" something other than an empirical claim in (desperate?) search of empirical justification.

Second: The Wittgensteinian defense of the major questions doctrine will not be sufficient in cases in which the court thinks (1) that the agency's claim of statutory authorization is more likely than not to be right but (2) the agency's claim of statutory authorization is not clearly right. In such cases, Justice Gorsuch would contend that the agency should lose. Justice Barrett obviously disagrees on that score. In her view, the idea of a new substantive canon, in the form of the major questions doctrine, is legally unmoored. Its creation cannot be squared with textualism; it lacks sources in any legal text or in tradition. And some people (probably not Justice Barrett) would add that the nondelegation doctrine, as Justice Gorsuch understands it, itself has dubious constitutional roots,[56] which raises a serious problem for his justification of the major questions doctrine (though not for Justice Barrett's).

Here is one effort at accommodation: The Avoidance Canon is a clear-statement principle, and no one should object to its status as such. And if an agency argues in favor of an interpretation that would be absurd, that interpretation should be rejected.[57] No one should object to the status of the Absurdity Canon as a clear-statement principle.[58] Patently unreasonable interpretations should also be rejected, unless Congress has clearly authorized them.[59] If an agency argues in favor of an interpretation that would raise a serious nondelegation problem, then that interpretation should be rejected.[60] And if an agency argues in favor of an interpretation that really would be "startling"—perhaps because it would produce a radical transformation in long-standing practice, perhaps because it would give the agency authority that no one had ever thought it had—then courts might reject that interpretation on Justice Barrett's ground, unless there is contextual evidence in favor of the agency's view. Such contextual evidence could include a broad term, such as *unreasonable risk* or *public interest*.[61]

That approach should give Justice Gorsuch, and those who approve of his approach, most of what they want. And under that approach, the major questions doctrine would have an important but well-defined role. It would not operate as a broad restriction on the authority of the executive branch. It need not be motivated by any large-scale doubts about the legitimacy of those agencies. It would be part of the judicial toolbox used, as Justice Barrett urges, as part of ordinary interpretation.

STEPPING BACK, STEPPING FORWARD

Is there any need for a major questions doctrine? I am not at all sure. We could readily imagine a parallel world, not so very different from ours, in which there was no such doctrine. It is reasonable to insist that this parallel

world was ours—certainly before the twenty-first century,[62] and perhaps
before 2023, when the doctrine was first announced.[63] In fact, *all the cases
now said to constitute the major question canon could have come out the same
way without the doctrine*. Almost all of the analysis in *Brown & Williamson*,
which helped originate the doctrine, focused on congressional instructions
and had nothing to do with the major questions doctrine.[64] The little seed
planted there seemed like an afterthought. Both *MCI* and *Biden v. Nebraska*
could have rested only on the ordinary meaning of the word *modify*.[65]
Indeed, the main thrust of both opinions was textualist and did not involve
the major questions doctrine at all.[66] *West Virginia* could easily have turned,
and largely did turn, on the court's interpretation of the relevant provision
of the Clean Air Act.[67] Something similar could be said about most and
perhaps all of the major questions cases, though they would be a bit easier
with the help of the Wittgensteinian argument.

In this light, the major questions doctrine seems a little like a make-
weight, which raises serious questions: What is the court doing with it?
Why does the court need it? Why has the court essentially invented it?

Justice Gorsuch gives the clearest answer: Some members of the court
appear gravely concerned, from the standpoint of separation of powers,
about the idea of a discretion-wielding executive branch, seizing on ambiguous language to take action that Congress did not specifically authorize.[68]
More generally, some members of the court appear to have serious constitutional doubts about the administrative state in its current form. From that
point of view, the major questions doctrine is an important way of maintaining faith with original constitutional commitments. It is connected
with the Grand Narrative. As such, and for reasons sketched earlier, I do
not embrace it, but we can recognize and honor its motivations.

Justice Barrett lightly makes a similar point[69] and may have a broadly
similar motivation, but her Wittgensteinian analysis certainly lowers the
volume on the debate. Whatever the justification for the major questions
doctrine, it would have a role to play in cases in which the agency's interpretation is either reasonable or right, given the traditional sources of statutory interpretation, but in which the extraordinary or startling nature
of the agency's action requires either (1) clear contextual support (Justice
Barrett's approach) or (2) clear congressional authorization (Justice Gorsuch's approach). The line between approaches 1 and 2 would appear to be
very thin.

We could readily imagine decisions, in the Supreme Court and in the lower courts, that do not choose between Justice Gorsuch and Justice Barrett and that reflect an incompletely theorized agreement on behalf of the major questions doctrine.[70] In most cases, the different justifications will not lead to different outcomes. Both the Biden administration and the Trump administration should lose significant cases. Justice Gorsuch and Justice Barrett agree with all the various cases now taken to constitute the doctrine, and while some of those cases tend to lean toward Justice Gorsuch's position,[71] they cannot easily be read to make an authoritative decision between them. As I have noted, the different analyses will usually produce the same outcome.

Enough about the trees; here is the forest. The major questions doctrine is a recent creation, but insofar as it is designed to ensure clear congressional authorization for transformative or previously unheralded action from the executive branch, it is rooted in the old idea of legislative primacy. It is a nondelegation canon. If it is subject to reasonable dispute, on the ground that it is a concoction that is ill-suited to the realities of modern government, then at least we can celebrate its insistence on the primacy of Congress with respect to the making of federal law. And insofar as it puts Congress in the driver's seat, and respects clear congressional instructions, it is unlikely to do a lot of harm. It might even do a lot of good.

11 ARMS CONTROL IS HARD

We have encountered James Bradley Thayer, who argued in favor of a sharply limited role for courts in a democratic society.[1] Thayer had a particular view of the separation of powers, one in which the courts would not do a whole lot. In modern terms, he can be seen as arguing for a kind of arms control agreement, in which judges would lay down their weapons. His argument failed. That failure contains large lessons about arms control agreements and about what ails many nations today.

Thayer urged that in the face of a constitutional challenge, all reasonable doubts should be resolved favorably to Congress, in the sense that the Constitution should be interpreted in a way that gives the political process maximum room to maneuver.[2] Justice Oliver Wendell Holmes offered one summary of the implications of Thayer's position (and wholeheartedly embraced it): "If my fellow citizens want to go to Hell I will help them. It's my job."[3] But Thayer was less pithy and more optimistic. He did not speak of going to Hell. He had faith in the democratic process.

Thayer began his essay with a large puzzle: "How did our American doctrine, which allows to the judiciary the power to declare legislative Acts unconstitutional, and to treat them as null, come about, and what is the true scope of it?"[4] In Thayer's view, this power cannot be justified by the mere fact that the Constitution is written: "So far as the grounds for this remarkable power are found in the mere fact of a constitution being in writing, or in judges being sworn to support it, they are quite inadequate. Neither the written form nor the oath of the judges necessarily involves the right of reversing, displacing, or disregarding any action of the legislature or the executive which these departments are constitutionally authorized to take, or the determination of those departments that they are so authorized."[5]

This is, of course, a swipe at Chief Justice John Marshall's opinion in *Marbury v. Madison*,[6] which emphasized the written nature of the Constitution and the importance of the oath. The "remarkable practice" of judicial review, as Thayer called it, was a product not of logic but of experience, and in particular "a natural result of our political experience before the War of Independence."[7] Great Britain had an external sovereign; the United States did not. In the United States, "our own home population in the several States were now their own sovereign. So far as existing institutions were left untouched, they were construed by translating the name and style of the English sovereign into that of our new ruler,—ourselves, the People."[8] For this reason, the new (state) constitutions "were precepts from the people themselves who were to be governed, addressed to each of their own number, and especially to those who were charged with the duty of conducting the government."[9] Judges enforced those precepts in the interest of protecting the sovereignty of the people against public officials.

This is what happened, but as Thayer saw it, it was hardly inevitable, and it was not clearly mandated by the Constitution itself. Thayer found it "instructive to see that this new application of judicial power was not universally assented to. It was denied by several members of the Federal convention, and was referred to as unsettled by various judges in the last two decades of the last century."[10] In the founding period, the power of judicial review was sharply disputed.

As that power emerged and became entrenched, "its whole scope was this; namely, to determine, for the mere purpose of deciding a litigated question properly submitted to the court, whether a particular disputed exercise of power was forbidden by the constitution."[11] In a crucial passage, Thayer said that such questions "require an allowance to be made by the judges for the vast and not definable range of legislative power and choice, for that wide margin of considerations which address themselves only to the practical judgment of a legislative body. Within that margin, as among all these legislative considerations, the constitutional law-makers must be allowed a free foot."[12]

The idea of a *free foot* was supported, in Thayer's account, by an insistence that the legislature *cannot act without initially making its own determination of constitutionality*. Thayer thought it "plain that where a power so

momentous as this primary authority to interpret is given, the actual deter-
minations of the body to whom it is entrusted are entitled to a correspond-
ing respect; and this not on mere grounds of courtesy or conventional
respect, but on very solid and significant grounds of policy and law."[13]
Thayer had no patience for the view that courts have "the mere and simple
office of construing two writings and comparing one with another, as two
contracts or two statutes are construed and compared when they are said
to conflict; of declaring the true meaning of each, and, if they are opposed
to each other, of carrying into effect the constitution as being of superior
obligation, an ordinary and humble judicial duty, as the courts sometimes
describe it."[14] In Thayer's account, this "way of putting it easily results in
the wrong kind of disregard of legislative consideration."[15]

Under the right approach, by contrast, "an Act of the legislature is not
to be declared void unless the violation of the constitution is so manifest
as to leave no room for reasonable doubt."[16] Thayer urged that this idea was
established "very early" and, in fact, became entrenched by 1811.[17] What
was necessary, for invalidation, was "a clear and unequivocal breach of the
Constitution, not a doubtful and argumentative implication."[18] As Thayer
put it, courts "can only disregard the Act when those who have the right
to make laws have not merely made a mistake, but have made a very clear
one,—so clear that it is not open to rational question."[19] Like any good
lawyer, Thayer urged not only that this approach is right but also that it
was and had long been, in fact, the prevailing view: "That is the standard
of duty to which the courts bring legislative Acts; that is the test which
they apply,—not merely their own judgment as to constitutionality, but
their conclusion as to what judgment is permissible to another department
which the constitution has charged with the duty of making it."[20]

In Thayer's account, "virtue, sense, and competent knowledge are always
to be attributed to" the national legislature.[21] It follows that whatever choice
is rational is constitutional. An "irrational excess" is unacceptable, but the
judicial role "is a secondary one."[22] As Thayer had it, "I am not stating a
new doctrine, but attempting to restate more exactly and truly an admitted
one."[23] This was his (bold) conception of the separation of powers.

Thayer believed that over time admitted doctrine would become even
more entrenched, for it is "a test, it may be added, that come[s] into more
and more prominence as our jurisprudence grows more intricate and
refined."[24] (Writing 12 years before *Lochner v. New York*,[25] 61 years before

Bolling v. Sharpe,[26] and 136 years before *Citizens United v. FEC*,[27] Thayer cannot be counted as a prophet.) Thayer was keenly alert to the claim that interpretation of the Constitution is a judicial act, not a legislative one. His response was that "a court cannot always, and for the purpose of all sorts of questions, say that there is but one right and permissible way of construing the constitution."[28] To strike down legislation, courts must be clear that it is invalid "beyond a reasonable doubt."[29]

Thayer concluded with some notes about the beneficial systemic consequences of his approach. One risk of judicial review is that it might serve "to drive out questions of justice and right, and to fill the mind of legislators with thoughts of mere legality, of what the constitution allows."[30] In these circumstances, "the safe and permanent road towards reform is that of impressing upon our people a far stronger sense than they have of the great range of possible harm and evil that our system leaves open, and must leave open, to the legislatures, and of the clear limits of judicial power; so that responsibility may be brought sharply home where it belongs."[31]

That is important because "under no system can the power of courts go far to save a people from ruin; our chief protection lies elsewhere. If this be true, it is of the greatest public importance to put the matter in its true light."[32] One of Thayer's evident goals was to activate political rather than judicial safeguards—to drive in, so to speak, consideration of justice and right. With respect to the separation of powers, Thayer had a reform project.

There is a clear link between Thayer's claims here and some famous words from Judge Learned Hand: "Liberty lies in the hearts of men and women; when it dies there, no constitution, no law, no court can even do much to help it. While it lies there it needs no constitution, no law, no court to save it."[33] Thayer's essay had a large impact on many readers. According to Justice Felix Frankfurter's biographer, "After he had read Thayer's essay, Frankfurter never stopped quoting it," and he "embraced Thayer's theory of limited judicial review and deference to elected officials in all but the most extreme circumstances."[34] According to Frankfurter himself, Thayer's was "the most important single essay" about American constitutional law, and "the great guide for judges."[35]

SCOPE

To be sure, there are lurking questions about the proper *scope* of Thayerism. A judge could be an across-the-board Thayerian, applying the "beyond a reasonable doubt" test whenever a constitutional challenge is raised. A judge could be a Thayerian for Congress, but not for the executive branch. A judge could be a Thayerian for Congress, but not for the states. In a brief and somewhat puzzling discussion, Thayer himself suggested that Congress, as a coordinate branch of government, should be subject to the beyond-a-reasonable-doubt test, but that states should not be: "If a State legislature passes a law which is impeached in the due course of litigation before the national courts, as being in conflict with the supreme law of the land, those courts may ask themselves a question different from that which would be applicable if the enactments were those of a co-ordinate department."[36]

But why? Thayer emphasized that in such cases, the federal courts are "representing a paramount constitution and government" and that they must "guard it from any inroads from without."[37] That's fair enough, but why does that call for something other than the beyond-a-reasonable-doubt standard? In what sense are states "from without"? Thayer did not answer these questions, and Thayer's followers, including Holmes, Brandeis, and Frankfurter, generally did not distinguish between federal and state legislation.

For present purposes, I will bracket Thayer's suggestion to this effect and treat Thayerism as an across-the-board idea.

INTERPRETATION

For all its importance, the Thayerian approach is radically incomplete. We have seen that to know whether a constitutional violation is clear, we need a theory of interpretation to help us understand what the Constitution means. We could imagine Thayerian textualists, who would uphold statutes and regulations against constitutional challenge unless there is, beyond a reasonable doubt, a violation of the text of the founding document. Under Thayerian textualism, it would be unconstitutional for Congress to enact a law establishing that the nation will have two presidents, or four, or twelve; the Constitution unambiguously creates a president. But under Thayerian textualism, it would not be unconstitutional to create independent agencies, whose heads could be discharged by the president only "for cause"; the text of the Constitution is not unambiguous on this question. Under Thayerian textualism, Congress could certainly discriminate on the basis of race and sex; that is straightforward. Under Thayerian textualism, the legislative veto would be constitutional; that is also straightforward.

We could also imagine Thayerian originalists, who would uphold statutes and regulations against constitutional attack unless the violation of the document, on the correct originalist reading, was clear. To be sure, originalists would want to ask some hard questions about Thayerism and above all, this one: Is Thayerism itself part of, or consistent with, the original public meaning? For originalists, Thayerism would seem to stand or fall on the answer to that question. Although it might be challenging to answer it as a matter of history, the consequences of Thayerian originalism are numerous, and many of them are straightforward. Under Thayerian originalism, for example, Congress could not impose prior restraints on speech, at least as a general rule; the original understanding of the First Amendment is (clearly) inconsistent with prior restraints.[38]

Under Thayerian originalism, there is an argument that the First Amendment would not forbid blasphemy laws.[39] Under Thayerian originalism, there would be no substantive due process under either the Fifth or Fourteenth Amendments.[40] (This conclusion depends on the more-than-plausible claim that that even if there is an originalist argument in favor of substantive due process, it is not clear beyond a reasonable doubt.)

We could easily imagine nonoriginalist Thayerians, who might (for example) believe that the Constitution should be given a moral reading,[41] but also that courts should uphold the decisions of the democratic branches unless the violation of the (best) moral reading was very clear. For example, nonoriginalist Thayerians might believe that the best moral reading of the Equal Protection Clause forbids affirmative action, but also that the issue is not straightforward, which would mean that affirmative action programs should be upheld.

We could imagine Thayerian common good constitutionalists,[42] who would insist that the Constitution should be understood in light of principles associated with the common good, but who would uphold legislation unless the transgression of those principles is entirely clear. Common good constitutionalists might believe, for example, that the best reading of the founding document does not allow states to authorize abortion, but also that reasonable people can disagree with that reading, which means that states can authorize abortion.

We could easily imagine Thayerian or Thayer-inspired minimalists, who would emphasize the importance of leaving things undecided—perhaps by using the passive virtues,[43] perhaps by ruling narrowly and shallowly.[44] Alexander Bickel, a champion of the passive virtues, did not embrace Thayerism, but he was evidently influenced and even haunted by it.[45] His great book on judicial review contains an entire section on Thayer's essay, which he calls "a singularly important piece of American legal scholarship, if for no other reason than that Holmes and Brandeis, among modern judges, carried its influence with them to the Bench, as more recently did Mr. Justice Frankfurter."[46] Bickel's enthusiasm for judicial silence, maintained by use of justiciability doctrines, has a distinctly Thayerian feel.

We could also imagine Thayerians of a more extreme sort, who would uphold legislation if, under *any* reasonable theory of constitutional interpretation, it is not unconstitutional beyond a reasonable doubt. For such Thayerians, the best approach would be to use the most permissive theory of interpretation and to ask if the relevant legislation is unambiguously inconsistent with that theory. In general, textualism might well be the most permissive approach to interpretation, in the sense that the constitutional text, by itself, often allows reasonable doubts with respect to a very wide range of possible understandings.

What is clear is that to operate at all, Thayerism must build on some independent theory of interpretation. What is also clear is that after it is thus built, we will find three categories of cases. In countless cases, Thayerism will offer a bright green light; the argument for constitutional invalidation will be preposterous. In a few cases, Thayerism will offer a red light; the constitutional violation is unambiguous. In a few cases, reasonable people will disagree about whether Thayerism authorizes or compels invalidation; there will be reasonable disagreement about whether the violation can be shown beyond a reasonable doubt.

THE PURSUIT OF NEUTRALITY

For contemporary constitutional law, and indeed for the constitutional law of the last century, the implications of Thayerism are not obscure. Suppose that a state prohibited abortion or same-sex marriage, required affirmative action, or imposed the death penalty. Thayerians would uphold those actions. Or suppose that Congress granted open-ended discretionary authority to regulatory agencies, enacted some successor to the Affordable Care Act under the Commerce Clause, or protected or prohibited abortion under section 5 of the Fourteenth Amendment. Thayerians would not be at all sympathetic to constitutional objections.

As these examples suggest, Thayerism has a kind of neutrality, which might well be taken as a point in its favor. It calls for judicial modesty, whether the measure in question is challenged by the left or the right. But it is revealing that in the long history of American law, it is exceedingly difficult to find across-the-board Thayerians. Holmes might have been the closest.[47] He voted consistently in favor of minimum wage and maximum hour laws, and other regulations involving the labor market. In his celebrated words, "The Fourteenth Amendment does not enact Mr. Herbert Spencer's Social Statics."[48]

He also voted in favor of compulsory sterilization laws. In his notorious words, "Three generations of imbeciles are enough."[49] The only clear exception to Holmes's Thayerism involves free speech,[50] and even there, he was a complex figure, shifting away from First Amendment Thayerism over time.[51] Justice Felix Frankfurter, who idolized Holmes, also idolized Thayer, and he understood himself as a Thayerian.[52] Indeed, there is an argument that Frankfurter was the last Thayerian on the Supreme Court.[53]

During his time on the court, Frankfurter's Thayerian inclinations created a great deal of tension with the legal and political left (he agreed with the latter as a matter of policy, but he was willing to vote to uphold a lot of things that he deplored).[54] At the same time, Frankfurter's complex record, and his important departures from Thayerism, raise numerous questions. Frankfurter was an architect of both *Brown v. Board of Education*[55] and *Bolling v. Sharpe*[56] and thus voted to strike down racial segregation; his commitment to Thayerism was qualified by his commitment to racial equality.[57]

Pointing to the traditions of English-speaking people, Frankfurter also embraced a "shock the conscience" test for due process violations, which consistent Thayerians would almost certainly reject. (Frankfurter called this the "make me puke" test, and he connected it with Holmes's own views.[58]) Still, Frankfurter's strong Thayerian inclinations led to sharp and pervasive disagreements with Justices William O. Douglas and Hugo Black.[59]

It is more than intriguing that after the demise of Lochnerism in the late 1930s,[60] and the rise of what seemed to be general enthusiasm for Thayerism in the 1940s and after,[61] New Deal participants and enthusiasts, once on the bench, quickly departed from Thayerism in the interest of values and principles prized by the left. Focusing on free speech, race discrimination, voting rights, and criminal justice, Justice Douglas departed from Thayerism regularly and without the slightest hesitation; Frankfurter did so far less frequently and with considerable soul-searching and agitation. We might even say that there was a window of opportunity, in the late 1930s and early 1940s, for a kind of entrenchment of Thayerism on the Supreme Court. For reasons that include (but are not limited to) the selection process and a degree of serendipity, that particular window closed fairly rapidly.[62]

TWO OWLS OF MINERVA, FLYING AT NIGHT

As a matter of principle, Alexander Bickel and John Hart Ely offer some clues about why the closing of that window was not much lamented at the time. Writing in 1962, and with *Brown*, *Bolling*, and McCarthyism evidently on his mind, Bickel rejected Thayerism. He noted Felix Cohen's suggestion that Thayer's approach would make "of our courts lunacy commissions sitting in judgment upon the mental capacity of legislatures."[63] Bickel did not endorse that characterization, but he was affected by it, and he responded that Thayer's approach "is not addressed . . . to all the problems faced by the process as it has operated in our day. Not nearly."[64] Bickel believed that "Thayer's rule tends to break down" when individual rights are at risk.[65]

One reason is that it "does not take a lunatic legislature to enact measures that are irrational"; a legislature that is "more than normally whipped up" might do the same.[66] In any case, the question may not be whether a legislative "accommodation is rational. The question may be whether it is good."[67] Pointing to restrictions on the use of birth control within marriage, Bickel said that the legislative judgment in favor of such restrictions "cannot be deemed irrational."[68] But because it applies to "conjugal privacy," Bickel suggested agreement with Justice John Marshall Harlan's suggestion that rationality was not enough; an "additional judgment to the one opened up by the rule of the clear mistake is called for."[69] In Bickel's account, Thayerism is "simply not enough."[70]

We can easily see why Bickel, writing in the early 1960s, would think that. In the end, Bickel insisted that judges "have, or should have, the leisure, the training, and the insulation to follow the ways of the scholar in pursuing the ends of government," which is "crucial in sorting out the enduring values of a society."[71] Bickel thought that the distinctive judicial role was to discern and insist on principles, because courts have "the capacity to appeal to men's better natures, to call forth their aspirations, which may have been forgotten in the moment's hue and cry."[72] To say the least, Bickel rejected Thayerism and did not contemplate a beyond-a-reasonable-doubt standard here, and he did not claim that the relevant principles were in any simple sense "in" the Constitution. The judges' task was to identify (or construct or specify) them.[73]

Writing in 1981, with a lot more non-Thayerian water under the constitutional bridge (or over the constitutional dam), Ely dedicated his book to Chief Justice Earl Warren: "You don't need many heroes if you choose carefully."[74] Chief Justice Warren was not a Thayerian by any means. But in Ely's account, he was committed to democracy, and he understood the role of the Supreme Court by reference to that commitment. Ely's view easily can be seen as an elaboration of the most famous footnote in all of American constitutional law—footnote 4 in *United States v. Carolene Products*,[75] which said, in relevant part:

> It is unnecessary to consider now whether legislation which restricts those political processes which can ordinarily be expected to bring about repeal of undesirable legislation, is to be subjected to more exacting judicial scrutiny under the general prohibitions of the Fourteenth Amendment than are most other types of legislation [referring to "restrictions upon the right to vote"; "restraints upon the dissemination of information"; "interferences with political organizations"; and "prohibition of peaceable assembly"].
>
> Nor need we enquire whether similar considerations enter into the review of statutes directed at particular religious, or national, or racial minorities; whether prejudice against discrete and insular minorities may be a special condition, which tends seriously to curtail the operation of those political processes ordinarily to be relied upon to protect minorities, and which may call for a correspondingly more searching judicial inquiry.[76]

To say the least, that is a serious qualification of Thayerism. In Ely's view, the Constitution should be interpreted in a way that makes the democratic process work as well as possible and that makes up for deficits in it. Above all, Ely urged that courts should vigorously protect democracy itself. One way to do that is to safeguard the franchise.[77] The idea of "one person, one vote" does, in Ely's view, have a solid constitutional justification, whether or not it finds support in any form of textualism or originalism. Ely also believed that courts do well to strike down poll taxes and restrictions on access to the polls.

To protect democracy, Ely argued in favor of an emphatically non-Thayerian judicial role in protecting political speech. For the same reason, he did not believe that the Constitution stands in the way of reasonable restrictions on campaign finance. In his view, such restrictions promote self-government; they do not undermine it.

Ely urged as well that courts should protect those who are at a systematic disadvantage in the political process, including Black people and noncitizens. This too is, of course, emphatically non-Thayerian. The reason for the protection is to compensate for systematic imperfections or deficits in democratic processes and hence to engage in a kind of democracy-reinforcing constitutional law. Departing dramatically from Thayer, Ely approved of the idea of "strict scrutiny" of any law that discriminates on the basis of race—with the important qualification that he would have no trouble with affirmative action, on the theory that on that issue, the democratic process can be trusted, because white people are not at a systematic disadvantage. On all of these counts, Ely endorsed a distinctive understanding of the separation of powers, in which courts would exercise far more authority than Thayer would allow.

At the same time, Ely would allow the democratic process a great deal of room to maneuver, so long as the process is functioning well. To that extent, he was a selective Thayerian. Ely had nothing to say in favor of *Roe v. Wade*. In fact, he firmly rejected it. He was sharply critical of the right to privacy and of any judicial effort to identify and protect what judges see as "fundamental values."

NO THAYERIANS HERE

The failure to adopt Thayerism in the 1930s and 1940s finds a parallel with the period from the 1970s to the present, in which Republican presidents, deeply unhappy with the emphatically non-Thayerian approach of the Warren court, succeeded in appointing numerous justices to the court. It would not be implausible to think that in some of those decades, there was another, perhaps golden window of opportunity for Thayerism, in which the court might have moved toward something like a beyond-a-reasonable-doubt test for constitutionality. But that did not happen. Strikingly,[78] there was no serious effort, on the part of one or more of the justices, to initiate such a movement.

In the modern era, there are no consistent Thayerians, and with the possible exception of Justice Stephen Breyer, no recent member of the court can be said to have much (general) sympathy for Thayerism. Some left-of-center justices are Thayerians with respect to the Second Amendment—but not with respect to sex discrimination. Some right-of-center justices are Thayerians with respect to abortion—but not with respect to the Second Amendment.

The court's originalists are emphatically not Thayerians;[79] they do not say that acts of Congress will be upheld unless the deviation from the original public meaning is unambiguous or unless Congress has deviated from it "beyond a reasonable doubt." They ask instead: Did Congress deviate from the original public meaning, in the court's independent view of the original public meaning? If they were genuine Thayerians, they would have had to agree that the Second Amendment does not protect the right to possess firearms; that restrictions on commercial advertising are not constitutionally vulnerable; that affirmative action programs are constitutionally fine.

Nor can the court's nonoriginalists be counted as Thayerians. They do not ask: Has there been a clear departure from the First Amendment, the Due Process Clause, or the Equal Protection Clause, given their preferred theory of interpretation? If they were Thayerians, they would have had to agree that the Constitution does not contain a right to privacy; that sex discrimination is constitutionally unobjectionable; that the federal government can engage in racial discrimination, including racial segregation; and that the government does not have to give procedural safeguards to those seeking to retain welfare benefits.

RIGHT AND LEFT

At some points in American history, Thayerism has had a strong appeal to the political right.[80] During the ascendancy of the Warren court, many conservatives rejected *judicial activism*, which they seemed to find in decisions striking down the actions of the democratic branches; consider, for example, the desegregation decisions and the idea of "one person, one vote." Conservatives wanted courts to be more deferential and hence more Thayerian. In recent decades, the left occasionally has shown far more interest in Thayerism or something like it (Thayerism adjacent), in evident response to rulings from the Supreme Court that seem, to the left, to be unfortunate or outrageous.[81]

On numerous occasions, the left has explored ways to limit the place of the Supreme Court in American life. One version of left-of-center Thayerism is a belief in *popular constitutionalism,* which sometimes takes the form of a rejection of the power of judicial review altogether.[82] In the current period, this kind of Thayerism, or Thayerism on steroids, seems to have considerable appeal in certain quarters.

There is a background point in support of left-wing Thayerism: It is often urged that as a matter of history, and as a matter of the likely future, the Supreme Court will reflect the political views of the powerful and the wealthy (as befits the fact that the justices are generally members of a political elite—lawyers with a potentially strong interest in the status quo). For those who embrace left-of-center Thayerism—whose extreme version seeks to eliminate the Supreme Court's power to invalidate legislation at all—the emblematic judicial decisions are those that

- strike down maximum hour and minimum wage laws;[83]
- protect the right to possess guns;[84]
- ban affirmative action programs;[85]
- strike down campaign finance regulation;[86]
- protect commercial advertising;[87]
- jeopardize the Patient Protection and Affordable Care Act;[88] and
- forbid regulation designed to protect safety, health, and the environment.[89]

If inadequate democracy is the problem, they think, then it is absurd to believe, with Ely, that the Supreme Court is the solution. Such Thayerians are deeply skeptical of originalism, which they regard as a mask for political preferences, and of the idea of any kind of free-form constitutional law (think: moral readings)—which, they believe, turn out to be reflections, often hidden, of an identifiable political agenda, one associated with the political right.

ATHENS AND BABEL

Should anyone embrace Thayerism? Today? Tomorrow? The day after? Is Thayerism a reasonable approach to the separation of powers?

Thayer understood his approach as an accurate description of practice. To say the least, it is no longer that, and to contemporary readers, Thayer's defense of Thayerism seems shockingly thin. He pointed to the supposed

fact that Congress must make a preliminary assessment of the constitutional question in order to enact law. But what does that mean, exactly? Is
it an empirical claim, or is it in some sense a logical necessity? If it is seen as
a logical necessity, then it is not clear why it is relevant. If it is an empirical
claim, then it is not clear that it was true when Thayer wrote, and it is not
at all clear that it is true now. If it is an empirical claim, and if it is true, then
it is not clear why it is relevant.

Suppose that Congress, with all its qualities and imperfections, makes a
judgment about the meaning of the Constitution. Why should courts treat
Congress as an expert tribunal on questions of constitutional law, subject
to something like review for arbitrariness? It cannot be because Congress
has particular expertise on the meaning of the Constitution, at least if that
meaning is thought to be accessible by standard legal means. As we have
seen, Congress's judgments about the meaning of the Constitution tend
to be motivated; members of Congress usually think that the Constitution
means what they want it to mean.

Recall that Thayerism would require courts to uphold almost all legislation—including school segregation in the District of Columbia, sex discrimination in federal employment, affirmative action, restrictions on abortion,
mandatory school prayer, restrictions on free speech, and much more. To
many people, that would not seem to be an appealing set of outcomes.
(And if it does, then we could come up with another list, one that might
not appeal at all.) But imagine a society—let us call it *Athens*—in which
democratic processes work exceedingly fairly and well, such that judicial
intervention is almost never required from the standpoint of anything that
really matters.[90] In Athens, racial segregation does not occur. Political processes are fair, and political speech is never banned. The legitimate claims
of religious minorities and property holders are respected. The systems of
federalism and separation of powers are safeguarded, precisely to the right
extent, by democratic institutions.[91]

Imagine, too, that in Athens, judges are tyrants, and their judgments are
highly unreliable. From the standpoint of political morality, judges make
systematic blunders when they attempt to give content to constitutional
terms such as *equal protection of the laws* and *due process of law*. By resolving constitutional questions without respecting the views of the legislature,
courts would make society worse, because their understandings of rights
and institutions are so bad.

In Athens, a Thayerian approach to the Constitution would make a great deal of sense, and judges should be persuaded to adopt it. These are extreme assumptions, of course, but even if they are softened significantly, the argument for a Thayerian approach might be convincing, all things considered.

By contrast, consider a society—let us call it *Babel*—in which democratic processes work poorly, in the sense that they do not live up to democratic ideals, and in which political majorities invade fundamental rights (say, freedom of religion and freedom of speech). Suppose that in Babel, judges are trustworthy, in the sense that they can make democratic processes work better (say, by safeguarding the right to vote), and that they can protect fundamental rights as they really should be understood. In Babel, the argument for Thayerism would not be plausible.

It follows that the arguments for or against Thayerism must turn on judgments, or informed hunches, about the likely performance of various institutions. We might accept Thayerism if we thought that in the long haul, our nation would be close enough to Athens. We might reject Thayerism if we thought that in the long haul, it would look much more like Babel. For one or another reason, we might be selective Thayerians. As we have seen, Ely was a prominent example. In general, he favored a deferential judicial role, but not where the democratic process was not functioning well, perhaps because the right to vote was being compromised.[92]

Whether or not Ely was right, the broader lesson is that no approach to constitutional law can be adopted or rejected in the absence of an answer to the question of whether it would make our constitutional order better rather than worse, which requires in turn a set of judgments about the likely behavior of various institutions. Thayer, Holmes, Hand, Brandeis, Cardozo, and Frankfurter all appear not to have recognized this point; their views about the appropriate judicial role rested on abstractions.

THAYER'S ARROWS

Thayerians do have two other arrows in their quiver. Recall the first, emphasized by Thayer himself, which is that in enacting legislation, Congress has already engaged the constitutional question and answered it. As we have seen, it is not clear whether that is a logical claim or an empirical one. If it is a logical claim, not resting on any fact, what relevance does it have? If it is an empirical claim, what is the evidence for it? And why, exactly, is it relevant?

Contemporary or future Thayerians might emphasize the systemic point pressed by Thayer himself. This is the second Thayerian arrow: If courts answer the constitutional question on their own, they might reduce the incentive of legislatures to think long and hard about questions of justice and morality. They will not ask, "Is this right?" They will ask instead, "Will courts uphold this?" If courts assess the constitutional issue independently, they might weaken the incentive of other officials, including legislators, to try to assess that issue. They might create a culture in which officials believe that the Constitution is distinctly and uniquely for courts. That would be an inferior culture.

These are not implausible claims, but we do not know the magnitude of the effect, and we do not even know the sign. If courts decide constitutional questions independently, will public officials put issues of morality and justice to one side? It is hardly clear that this has happened or will happen. Whether legislators attend to issues of morality and justice depends on a lot of things; it would not seem to depend on whether courts are or are not Thayerian. If courts do not follow Thayer, will public officials pay less attention to the Constitution? It is hardly clear that this has happened or will happen. Indeed, an independent judicial role might lead officials to pay *more* rather than less attention to constitutional requirements. It might intensify attention to those requirements. After all, legislators do not want courts to strike down their handiwork.

ARMS CONTROL IS HARD

We might understand Thayerism as a proposal for a kind of arms control agreement: *I will adopt a Thayerian approach if you will as well*. More particularly, left-of-center judges might be willing to be Thayerian if and only if right-of-center judges are willing to be Thayerian as well. We could understand the situation in the terms of game theory. For purposes of simplification, assume that left-of-center judges have this preference ordering: (1) left-of-center results, (2) Thayerism, (3) right-of-center results. Right-of-center judges might have this preference ordering: (1) right-of-center results, (2) Thayerism, (3) left-of-center results.[93] We could imagine an agreement on option (2). That agreement would be more likely, of course, if there is keen interest in Thayerism in principle, in the form of a belief that it is right, appealing, or at least reasonable.

History suggests that no agreement in favor of option (2) is achievable. One problem is that at any given moment, both sides might have the votes to get option (1). The broader problem is that unless a strong Thayerian norm is internalized and in place, both sides will be tempted to defect. And that is, in fact, what we observe.

But my main conclusion lies elsewhere. Thayerism cannot be accepted or rejected in the abstract. It cannot be read off high ideals. Any approach to constitutional law, including the separation of powers, must be defended on the ground that it would make our constitutional order better rather than worse, which requires in turn a set of judgments about the likely behavior of various institutions. In my view, Thayerism would make our system worse. By greatly weakening the role of courts, it would undermine the system of separated powers.

12 PARTYISM

With respect to prejudice and hostility, the English language has many isms. Racism, sexism, classism, and speciesism are prominent examples. I aim to coin a new one here: *partyism*. The central idea is that merely by identifying with a political party, a person becomes enthusiastic about his own party and hostile to the opposing party, and willing to believe that its members have a host of bad characteristics.[1]

Partyism is real and on the rise, and it has serious harmful consequences for governance, politics, and daily life. Under conditions of severe partyism, a nation might find it difficult to address serious social problems, at least through legislation. To that extent, the system of separation of powers— which already imposes a series of barriers to legislative initiatives—becomes genuinely unsettled. Members of Congress often focus less on their own institutional prerogatives than on a different question: the prerogatives of their own party. As Daryl Levinson and Richard Pildes have emphasized, we see less in the way of separation of powers and more in the way of separation of parties.[2] Under President Biden, Democrats in Congress might think, "I will do as the president wants," while Republicans might think, "I will do the opposite of what the president wants." Under President Trump, Republicans might support whatever the president supports ("Yes sir!"), while Democrats might reject whatever the president supports ("Absolutely not!"). Partyism causes real harm. It can endanger liberty, and it can endanger deliberative democracy.

UH-OH

There is a great deal of evidence of partyism and its growth. Perhaps the simplest involves *thermometer ratings*.[3] For these ratings, people are asked to rate a range of groups on a scale of 1 to 100, where 100 means that the respondent feels "warm" toward the group and 0 means that the respondent feels "cold." In-party rankings remained stable over the last decades, with both Democrats and Republicans ranking members of their own party around 70. By contrast, ratings of the out-party experienced a remarkable fifteen-point dip in a short period.[4] In 2008, the average out-party ranking was around 30—and apparently declining.

By contrast, Republicans ranked "people on welfare" at 50 in that year, and Democrats ranked "Big Business" at 52. It is remarkable but true that negative affect toward the opposing party was not merely greater than negative affect toward unwelcome people and causes; it was much greater.

Consider one of the most influential measures of prejudice: the implicit association test (IAT).[5] The test is simple to take. Participants see words on the upper corners of a screen—for example, *white* paired with either *good* or *bad* in the upper-left corner, and *black* paired with one of those same adjectives in the upper right. Then they see a picture or a word in the middle of the screen—for example, a white face, an African American face, or the word *joy* or *terrible*. The task is to click on the upper corner that matches either the picture or the word in the middle.

Many white people quickly associate positive words like *joy*, or an evidently European American (Caucasian) face, with the upper-left corner when it says *white* and *good*—but have a much harder time associating *joy* with the upper-left corner when the words there are *black* and *good*.[6] So too do many white people quickly associate *terrible* with the upper-left corner when it says *black* and *bad*, but proceed a lot more slowly when the upper-left corner says *white* and *bad*.[7] And when the picture in the middle is evidently of a European American (Caucasian) face, white people are a lot faster in associating it with the word *good* than when the picture is evidently of an African American face.[8]

It is tempting to think that racial prejudice is deeply engrained and that nothing comparable can be found in the political domain, at least with respect to the two major parties in the United States. (To be sure, we might expect to see strongly negative implicit attitudes for *Nazis* or *Communists*.)

To test for political prejudice, Shanto Iyengar and Sean Westwood, political scientists at Stanford University, conducted a large-scale implicit association test with two thousand adults.[9] They found people's political bias to be much larger than their racial bias. When Democrats see *joy*, it is much easier for them to click on a corner that says *Democratic* and *good* than on one that says *Republican* and *good*. Implicit bias across racial lines remains significant, but it is significantly greater across political lines.[10]

Consider this: If you are a Democrat, would you marry a Republican? Would you be upset if your sister did?

Researchers have long asked such questions about race, and have found that along important dimensions, racial prejudice is decreasing.[11] At the same time, party prejudice in the US has jumped, infecting not only politics but also decisions about marriage. In 1960, just 5 percent of Republicans and 4 percent of Democrats said that they would feel "displeased" if their son or daughter married outside their political party.[12] By 2010, those numbers had reached 49 percent and 33 percent.[13] Interestingly, comparable increases cannot be found in the United Kingdom.[14]

In 2009, by contrast, 63 percent of Americans reported that they "would be fine" if a member of their family married someone of any other race or ethnicity, a sharp change from as recently as 1986, when 65 percent of respondents said that interracial marriage was not fine for anyone or not fine for them.[15] Asked specifically about marriages between African American and white partners, only 6 percent of white respondents and 3 percent of African Americans recently said that "they could not accept a black-white interracial marriage in their family."[16] Similarly, a Gallup survey found that 87 percent of people approve of interracial marriage, as opposed to 4 percent in 1958—a dramatic shift in social norms, showing the opposite trend line from that observed for partyism.[17]

HIRING

The IAT measures attitudes, not behavior. Growing disapproval of marriage across political lines suggests an increase in prejudice and hostility, but it might not map onto actual conduct. To investigate behavior, Iyengar and Westwood asked more than one thousand people to look at the résumés of several high school seniors and say which ones should be awarded a scholarship.[18] Some of these résumés contained explicitly racial cues (e.g., "president of the African American Student Association") while others had explicitly political ones (e.g., "president of the Young Republicans").[19]

In terms of ultimate judgments, race certainly mattered: African American participants preferred the African American scholarship candidates, 73 percent to 27 percent.[20] For their part, white people showed a modest preference for African American candidates as well, though by a significantly smaller margin.[21] But party affiliation made a much larger difference. Both Democrats and Republicans selected their in-party candidate about 80 percent of the time.[22] Even when a candidate from the opposing party had better credentials, most people chose the candidate from their own party.[23] With respect to race, in contrast, merit prevailed.[24] It is worth underlining this finding: *Racial preferences were eliminated when one candidate was clearly better than the other. By contrast, party preferences lead people to choose a clearly inferior candidate.*

A similar study asked students to play the role of college admissions director and to decide which applicants to invite for an on-campus interview, based on both objective criteria (SAT scores, class rank) and subjective evidence (teacher recommendations).[25] Among partisans with strong party identification, there was significant evidence of partyism: 44 percent of the participants reviewing someone from the opposite party selected the stronger applicant, while 79 percent of the participants in the control (where participants had no knowledge of the applicant's party affiliation) selected the stronger applicant.[26]

In a further test of the relationship between partyism and actual behavior, Iyengar and Westwood asked eight hundred people to play the *trust game*,[27] well-known among behavioral scientists.[28] As the game is played, Player 1 is given some money (say, $10) and told that she can give some, all, or none of it to Player 2. Player 1 is then told that the researcher will triple the amount that she allocates to Player 2—and that Player 2 can give some of that back to Player 1. When Player 1 decides how much money to give Player 2, a central question is how well she trusts him to return an equivalent or greater amount. Higher levels of trust will result in higher initial allocations.

Are people less willing to trust people of a different race or party affiliation? Iyengar and Westwood found that race did not matter—but party did. People are significantly more trusting of others who share their party affiliation.[29]

Partyism can motivate partisans to be especially inclined to share negative information about the opposing party—or even to avoid its members
altogether when forming a group.[30] In one experiment, participants were
asked to decide whether a strongly worded opinion piece blaming congressional gridlock on one of the two political parties, including hyperbole and
name-calling, should be posted on a news organization's website.[31] The
researchers found significant evidence of partyism: 65 percent of people
were willing to post the article if it was critical of the opposing party, but
only 25 percent were willing to share it if it criticized their own party.[32]
They also found that the intensity of a participant's partisan feelings correlated with their willingness to share a critical article.[33]

In a second experiment, the researchers asked participants to pick a team
of three people out of a list of four to join them in completing a puzzle
game.[34] Participants were informed of the partisan identity and education
level of the potential teammates; the least-educated team member was
always an independent. More than half the participants selected the least-
educated player for their team—rather than choosing a better-educated
member of the opposing party![35]

AN OBJECTION

From these studies, and various others,[36] it seems clear that partyism is
widespread in the United States. We can imagine reasonable disputes about
the precise magnitude of the phenomenon, but not about its existence and
significance. Still, there is an obvious objection to the effort to compare
racism to partyism, and indeed to the very effort to describe partyism as
seriously troubling. The objection is that people have legitimate reasons
for objecting to people because of their political beliefs. If we think that
Communism is hateful, we will not object to those who do not much like
Communists. "Red-baiting" is not exactly admirable, but it would not be
helpful to identify and to object to "Communismism."

For some people, a degree of suspicion and hostility across political lines
is a product of legitimate disagreement, not of anything untoward. Racism
and sexism are products of devaluation of human beings on the basis of a
morally irrelevant characteristic. Perhaps the same cannot be said for party
affiliation. In fact, the very idea of political prejudice, or any kind of corre-
sponding ism, might seem badly misdirected. Perhaps we are speaking here

not of any kind of prejudice, but of a considered judgment about people who hold certain convictions. On certain assumptions, that is the precise opposite of prejudice.

To come to terms with this response, we need to begin by distinguishing between daily life and politics as such. It is hardly unreasonable to have a strong negative affect toward Nazis or Communists because of their political views. But if people dislike each other because of an affiliation with one of the major parties in the United States, something does seem badly amiss. To be sure, some characteristics or even commitments of one or another party might seem troublesome or worse. But both parties are large and diverse, and it is odd to think that in general, members of one party should actually dislike members of another party as such.

Of course, this judgment turns on substantive conclusions. If you believe that Republicans are essentially racists and sexists, then antipathy toward Republicans is understandable, and so, too, if you believe that Democrats are unpatriotic socialists who hate the United States and want to undermine it. But if you believe that across the two parties, good-faith disagreements are possible and pervasive, then partyism will be hard to defend, not least if it seeps into daily life.

In the political domain, of course, intensely held differences are common, and some kind of us versus them attitude may be difficult or impossible to avoid. For members of Congress, some version of such an attitude is, in a sense, built into the very structure of the two-party system. A degree of antipathy—at least if it is not personal—may reflect principled disagreement, not prejudice at all. It may be hard to avoid a measure of antipathy with respect to people with whom you intensely disagree, most of the time, in your day job. The problem is that good faith disagreement is far from uncommon in politics, and in the face of such disagreement, the task is to seek to identify ways to move forward (or not), rather than to discredit arguments because of their source. With respect to politics itself, something like partyism may be a product of principle, but it also has destructive consequences, as we shall shortly see.

A little story: A few years ago, I had breakfast with two senators, one Republican and one Democrat, to try to make progress on an important topic that sharply divided the two parties. The senators worked well together; they seemed to like each other. I certainly liked both of them. At the breakfast, we did make some progress. After a few months, the two senators, and many Republican and Democratic members of Congress, developed and supported legislation that was exceedingly sensible and that would have made a big difference. Still, the legislation was killed. The reason? The long story is complicated, but the short story is just one word. Partyism.

Note well: Separation of powers did not make a lot of difference. Every-thing depended on partyism, and partyism is what made things hard and ultimately impossible.

CAUSES

What causes partyism? We do not yet know the answer, but some helpful clues have started to emerge.

FROM IDEOLOGICAL DISAGREEMENT TO PARTYISM?

It is tempting to think that the growth in partyism is a product of the increasing intensity and visibility of ideological disagreements. Let us assume that at some point in the past—say, 1970—one or another of the two parties, or perhaps both, had a "wider tent." Let us assume, in fact, that the conservative wing of the Democratic Party was more conservative than the liberal wing of the Republican Party, so that the two parties had significant ideological overlap. If so, we would not expect to see so much in the way of partyism.

This hypothesis could be tested in multiple ways. We could attempt to track ideological differences between the parties and test whether growth in ideological distance turned out to be correlated with increases in partyism. A strong correlation would not be definitive, but it would be at least sug-gestive. It would indicate that strong negative affect, across political lines, would have something to do with increasingly intense substantive disagree-ments. And if this turned out to be so, the rise of partyism would, in a sense, turn out to be rational, at least in the sense that prejudice and antipathy would be a product of something concrete and real. The role of partyism in the private domain might remain hard to defend (why would you dislike a nice neighbor who thought differently from you about climate change?), but in politics, at least, its recent increase would be comprehensible.

A better way to test the hypothesis might be to see whether the inten-sity of people's policy preferences predicts partyism. In other words: When people have very strong views about political issues (climate change, immigration, civil rights), and when those very strong views suggest clear divisions across party lines, are they more likely to show a negative affect toward the opposing party? Surprisingly, *the connection between ideological polarization and negative affect is relatively weak.*[37] It appears that people's partisan attachments are a product of their *identity* rather than their *ideology*. When Republicans dislike Democrats, or vice versa, it is largely because they are on the opposing side; substantive disagreements matter, to be sure, but they do not seem to be the primary drivers.

CAMPAIGNS

Do political campaigns create partyism? It is natural to suspect that they do, first because they make party differences salient, and second because part of the point is to cast people on the opposing side in a negative light—to show them as idiots or demons. Iyengar and Westwood find support for this hypothesis. In particular, exposure to negative advertising contributes to a growth in partisan animus, and political campaigns themselves have that effect.[38] Campaigns serve to "prime" partisan identity, and they also support stereotypical and negative perceptions of both supporters and opponents.

YOUR MEDIA, MY MEDIA

In a fragmented media market, it is easy for people to segregate along partisan lines. Fox News has an identifiable conservative orientation; MSNBC has an identifiable liberal orientation. Some talk shows are easy to characterize in terms of the political commitments of the host. If a show, a station, a podcast, a website, or a newsfeed characterizes one group of people as "the other side," and if those on that side are described as evil, foolish, or power hungry, then viewers or listeners should experience a rise in partyism.[39] We do not have definitive data on this particular speculation, though some good evidence is emerging,[40] and it is reasonable to suspect that a fragmented media market, with clear political identifications, contributes a great deal to partyism. Of course, social media platforms are a contributor here, and in my view, they are a significant one, though that is a topic for another occasion.

BAD CONSEQUENCES

Is partyism bad? We have focused on ordinary people, but of course many of the most relevant consequences are for governance. As I have suggested, and as Levinson and Pildes showed in that brilliant essay in 2015,[41] the separation of powers is now accompanied by, or displaced by, the separation of parties. The reason is that legislators often focus on a single question: *What is the political party of the president?* Much of the time, the answer to that question determines their behavior and their votes. To that extent, the separation of powers matters much less than party affiliation. We can identify three sets of bad consequences.

FEWER CHECKS

Most simply, the legislature does not check the executive if both are in the same partisan hands. Notice the formulation: It is not that the executive does not check the legislature if they are in the same partisan hands, though that might also be true. The executive usually takes the lead, and it is the most dangerous branch. Partyism means that the most dangerous branch is less likely to be constrained under conditions of one-party rule. That is an exceedingly serious problem.

To be sure, courts are independent, but party matters there as well. Judges nominated by Republican presidents are hardly lackeys, but they are more likely to rule in favor of Republican presidents than are Democratic appointees, and the converse is also true. That is also a serious problem. It is a threat to liberty and to self-government. Partyism raises the specter of authoritarianism.

POLARIZATION

Suppose that a society is divided on some proposition. The first group believes A, and the second group believes not-A. Suppose that the first group is correct. Suppose finally that truthful information is provided, not from members of the first group but from some independent source, in support of A. It would be reasonable to suppose that the second group would come to believe A. But in important settings, the opposite happens. The second group continues to believe not-A, and even more firmly than before. The result of the correction is to increase polarization.

The underlying studies do not involve party differences as such, but they explore something very close to that, and they suggest the following proposition: An important consequence of partyism is to ensure that *people with a strong political identification may be relatively immune from corrections, even on matters of fact, from people who do not share that identification.* Because agreement on matters of fact is often a precondition for political progress, this phenomenon can be extremely destructive.

In a relevant experiment, people were exposed to a mock news article in which President George W. Bush defended the Iraq war, in part by suggesting (as President Bush in fact did) that there "was a risk, a real risk, that Saddam Hussein would pass weapons or materials or information to terrorist networks."[42] After reading this article, they read about the Duelfer Report, which documented the lack of weapons of mass destruction in Iraq. Subjects were then asked to state their agreement, on a five-point scale (from "strongly agree" to "strongly disagree") with the statement that Iraq "had an active weapons of mass destruction program, the ability to produce these weapons, and large stockpiles of WMD."[43]

The effect of the correction greatly varied by political ideology. For very liberal subjects, there was a modest shift in favor of disagreement with this statement; the shift was not significant, because very liberal subjects already tended to disagree with it.[44] But for those who characterized themselves as conservative, there was a statistically significant shift in the direction of *agreeing* with the statement. "In other words, the correction backfired— conservatives who received a correction telling them that Iraq did not have WMD were more likely to believe that Iraq had WMD than those in the control condition."[45] It follows that the correction had a polarizing effect; it divided people more sharply, on the issue at hand, than they had been divided before.

An independent study confirmed the more general effect. People were asked to evaluate the proposition that cutting taxes is so effective in stimulating economic growth that it actually increases government revenue. They were then asked to read a correction. The correction increased some people's commitments to the proposition that had been corrected! "Conservatives presented with evidence that tax cuts do not increase government revenues ended up believing this claim more fervently than those who did not receive a correction."[46]

Or consider a test of whether apparently credible media corrections alter the belief, supported and pressed by former Alaska Governor Sarah Palin, that the Affordable Care Act would create "death panels."[47] Among those who viewed Palin favorably but had limited political knowledge, the correction succeeded; it also succeeded among those who viewed Palin unfavorably.[48] But the correction backfired among Palin supporters with a high degree of political knowledge. After receiving the correction, they became *more* likely to believe that the Affordable Care Act would create death panels.[49]

Liberals (and Democrats) are hardly immune to this effect. In 2005, many liberals wrongly believed that President George W. Bush had imposed a ban on stem cell research.[50] Presented with a correction from the *New York Times* or the Fox News website, liberals generally continued to believe what they did before.[51] By contrast, conservatives accepted the correction.[52] Hence, the correction produced an increase in polarization.

We do have to be careful with these findings. There is evidence that when the source of a correction is taken to be reliable, corrections can work.[53] The backfire effect occurs only under specific circumstances, which have yet to be clearly identified. It is plausible to speculate that when people have a strong emotional commitment to one or another view, a particularly credible source will be necessary to dislodge it. It is also plausible to speculate that when people think they have excellent reasons for a conviction, it will take a lot to get them to give up that conviction. The only point is that in important settings, corrections do not work and might backfire. Partyism is a reason.

Some of the experiments on the backfire effect involve people with clear ideological (rather than partisan) convictions; some of them focus on party affiliation. Indeed, an important and related study shows that people will follow the views of their party even when those views diverge from their independent judgments—and also that they are blind to the effects of party influence.[54]

In the relevant study, people—both Democrats and Republicans—were asked their views about some political issues. As a result, it was possible to obtain a sense of how members of both parties actually thought about those issues. Otherwise identical groups were then asked about exactly the same issues, but with one difference: They were informed of the views of party leadership. Some of those groups were told that the leadership of their party approved of a reform and that the leadership of the opposing party opposed it. Other groups were given the opposite information; they were told that the leadership of their party opposed the reform and that the leadership of the opposing party favored it. Different groups of Democrats and Republicans were subject to the two different conditions. The question was this: Would Democrats oppose a reform if and because the leadership of their party opposed it, and would they favor the same reform if and because the leadership of their party favored it? Would Republicans behave the same way?

The basic finding was that both Democrats and Republicans were massively affected by the views of their party leadership. Having learned what party leadership thought, people departed from the views that they would have held if they had not been so armed. Actually, they turned on a dime. Stunningly, the effect of information about the views of party leadership "overwhelmed the impact of both the policy's objective impact and participants' ideological beliefs."[55] At the same time, people were blind to that impact; they said that their judgments were based solely on the merits, not on the effects of learning about the beliefs of party leaders. Here, then, is clear evidence of the consequences of partyism for people's judgments—and of people's unawareness of that fact.

MORE GRIDLOCK?

It might be expected that under the circumstances of partyism, legislation would be difficult to enact. If legislators themselves suffer from partyism, then this conclusion should seem self-evident. And even if legislators do not suffer from partyism—even if they feel no antagonism to members of the opposing party, and are fully willing to work with them—then electoral pressures should push in the direction of gridlock. In fact, evidence suggests that partyism has often contributed to a highly unusual degree of inactivity in Congress.

This is especially likely to be true, of course, when government is divided. If the Senate or the House is controlled by Democrats, good luck to a Republican president! Under circumstances of one-party rule, in which the Senate, the House, and the White House are controlled by the same party. we might expect a flood of legislation. But if the opposing party will stick together, a degree of gridlock might occur even under those circumstances. If the House or Senate has roughly equal numbers from both parties, then the minority party just needs a few votes from the majority.

There is of course a legitimate question whether gridlock is good or bad. If an active Congress would do terrible things, there would be a good argument for an inactive Congress. The volume of activity is not the guide. A blocked national legislature is something to lament only if the result, all things considered, is to make things worse.

A full account of any particular state of affairs would require a theory of optimal deadlock, and this is not the place for any such theory. But it seems reasonable to think that if a nation faces a range of serious problems, if imaginable initiatives would reduce or solve those problems, and if partyism makes it difficult to undertake those initiatives, then something is badly amiss. Under imaginable assumptions, all those assumptions are reasonable.

GOOD NEWS

Partyism is compromising the system of separation of powers, but it is hardly eradicating it. I have said that it infects the relationship between the president and the judiciary, but the judiciary remains independent and operates as a crucial check. (Enough of a check? Probably not. An important check? Absolutely.) I have said that the legislature often follows the president if the two share a party affiliation, but even so, the legislature will have a minority party, which probably means that the president cannot simply get the legislation that he wants. (Ask Presidents Obama, Biden, and Trump.) Although the separation of powers is compromised by partyism, here is the good news: It is alive and well.

EPILOGUE

Return to 1933. "Chancellor, Pre-eminent Over Cabinet, Is Now Practically the German Government. All Legislative Powers Have Been Transferred to Regime, Free to Refashion National Life."

Nearly a hundred years afterward, some people are not so enthusiastic about references to Nazism and Germany, on the ground that they are too inflammatory and might load the analytical dice. But Hitler did receive legislative powers, and he did refashion national life. In the decades since his death, many people, and many leaders, have not been so enthusiastic about the idea of separation of powers. We do not have data, but worldwide enthusiasm for that idea appears to be a lot lower now than it was fifty years ago.

Why is that? One reason is that some problems really do need to be solved, and quickly rather than slowly. The separation of powers is not exactly a friend to rapid solutions. I know someone who visited Russia a few years ago for a meeting with President Vladimir Putin. Putin was late for the meeting, and my friend, who ran a large company, was afraid that she would miss her flight. There appeared to be no way for her to make it, given the traffic. Putin told her, "Don't worry, you'll make it." He gave her a government car, and he closed the relevant streets for her. She made the flight.

Every nation on the planet faces more serious problems than missed flights. If the goal is to address crime, immigration, air pollution, inflation, unemployment, or public health, a lot of people will want someone to be unencumbered, free to refashion national life.

Some people do not believe in separation of powers at all. They believe that it is a relic. They think that its costs outweigh its benefits. Other people do not go that far. They do not want to concentrate all power in a single person, but they think that standard understandings of the separation of powers are simply too restrictive and too rigid. They are open to many things: emergency powers for the national leader; considerable power, for the national leader, to bypass the legislature, when the need really is great; immunity for the national leader; considerable power, for the national leader, to bypass the courts.

Are these proposals good ones? There is no abstract answer, suitable for all times and places, to that question. Nothing in this book can be counted as an objection to the grant of a high degree of discretionary power to the president. Liberty has many faces, and it is plausible to say that people are less free if they are exposed to dirty air or water, or if they face unsafe working conditions. Freedom from violence requires government to be present, not absent. A weak state cannot protect liberty.

Even so, grave threats come from a government that is liberated from the constraints of the separation of powers. An executive that has lawmaking power can do a lot of good, but it can also produce horror (and it probably will). A legislature that exercises executive power is a recipe for tyranny. An independent judiciary needs to be available and able to hold the executive to account. An independent judiciary needs to be able to constrain the legislature as well—at a minimum, by interpreting the laws and (let us hope) by striking down those that offend the Constitution. An independent judiciary is critical, because it is an after-the-fact corrective to official lawlessness—and also a before-the-fact deterrent.

Separation of powers is a bet. It's the right bet.

ACKNOWLEDGMENTS

I am grateful to many people for help with this book, which reflects about a quarter century of work on the subject (and possibly more, depending on how you count). My decision to do a book on the subject had a great deal to do with events in the world; in many nations, including my own, the separation of powers is under siege.

Thanks first and foremost to my editor, Catherine Woods, who had the initial idea, and who made everything better. Thanks too to Sarah Chalfant, my agent, who was a terrific guide. Over the years, Jon Elster, Elizabeth Emens, Jack Goldsmith, Stephen Holmes, John Manning, Martha Nussbaum, Eric Posner, Sai Prakash, David Strauss, and Edna Ullmann-Margalit deserve particular thanks for ideas, comments, and suggestions. I am also grateful to four anonymous reviewers for many helpful suggestions.

I have drawn on previous essays here, while also substantially revising earlier discussions. For chapters 2, 3, and 4, I have drawn on *Separation of Powers Is a They, Not an It*, 48 Harv. J.L. & P.P. 149 (2024); for chapter 6, *The Most Knowledgeable Branch*, 164 U Pa. L. Rev. 1607 (2016); for chapter 7, *Deliberative Democracy In the Trenches*, 146 Daedalus 129 (2017); for chapter 8, *Administrative Law's Grand Narrative*, 72 Admin. L. Rev. 291 (2025); for chapter 9, *Nondelegation Canons*, 67 U. Chi. L. Rev 315 (2000); for chapter 10, *Two Justifications for the Major Questions Doctrine*, 76 Fla. L. Rev. 251 (2024); for chapter 11, *Thayerism*, U. Chi. L. Rev. Online (2024); and for chapter 12, *Partyism*, 2015 U. Chi L. Forum 1 (2015). Many thanks to each of the foregoing publications for permission to draw on that work here.

NOTES

CHAPTER 1

1. Guido Enderis, *Hitler Is Supreme Under Enabling Act*, N.Y. Times (Mar. 27, 1933), https://www.nytimes.com/1933/03/27/archives/hitler-is-supreme-under-enabling-act-chancellor-preeminent-over.html.

2. Id.

3. Id.

4. Detlev Vagts, *Carl Schmitt's Ultimate Emergency: The Night of the Long Knives*, 87 Germanic Rev. 203, 206 (2012).

5. See generally Phil Carradice, *Night of the Long Knives: Hitler's Excision of Rohm's SA Brownshirts, 30 June–2 July 1934* (2018).

6. Vagts, supra note 4, at 206.

7. Id.

8. Id.

9. U.S. Const. pmbl.

10. For versions of this view, see F. A. Hayek, *The Constitution of Liberty* (1960); and Richard A. Epstein, *Simple Rules for a Complex World* (1995).

11. See Hayek, supra note 10.

12. See generally Joseph M. Bessette, *The Mild Voice of Reason: Deliberative Democracy and American National Government* (1994).

13. See generally Gordon Wood, *The Radicalism of the American Revolution* (1992).

14. Abraham Lincoln, *Speech on the Kansas-Nebraska Act at Peoria, Illinois*, in *Abraham Lincoln: Speeches and Writings 1832–1858*, 307, 328 (1989) (emphasis added).

15. See generally Bessette, supra note 12; Cass R. Sunstein, *Interest Groups in American Public Law*, 38 Stan. L. Rev. 29 (1985); and *Deliberative Democracy* (Jon Elster ed., 1998).

16. See generally Jerry L. Mashaw, *Reasoned Administration and Democratic Legitimacy: How Administrative Law Supports Democratic Government* (2018).

17. *The Federalist No. 47*, at 298 (James Madison) (Clinton Rossiter ed., 2003).

18. U.S. Const. art. I, § 1.

19. U.S. Const. art. II, § 1.

20. U.S. Const. art. III, § 1.

21. See Cass R. Sunstein, *How to Interpret the Constitution* (2023), for discussion of many different views.

22. For a possible example, see Crowell v. Benson, 285 U.S. 22 (1932). The law has taken many twists and turns here. See Commodity Futures Trading Comm'n v. Schor, 478 U.S. 833 (1986); Thomas v. Union Carbide Agric. Prod. Co., 473 U.S. 568 (1985); SEC v. Jarkesy, 144 S. Ct. 2117 (2024).

23. See, for example, Lawrence Solum, *The Public Meaning Thesis: An Originalist Theory of Constitutional Meaning*, 101 B.U. L. Rev. 1953 (2021).

24. See, for example, Jed H. Shugerman, *The Indecisions of 1789: Inconstant Originalism and Strategic Ambiguity*, 171 U. Pa. L. Rev. 753 (2023); and Jerry L. Mashaw, *Creating the Administrative Constitution: The Lost One Hundred Years of American Administrative Law* (2012). On some big surprises, see generally Jonathan Gienapp, *Against Originalism: A Historical Critique* (2024)—arguing, among other things, that "the Constitution" was not understood, at the founding period, to be limited to the text.

25. See, for example, NLRB v. Noel Canning, 573 U.S. 513 (2014).

26. For a defining treatment, see M. J. C. Vile, *Constitutionalism and the Separation of Powers* (2d ed. 1998).

27. See *The Federalist No. 47*, at 299 (Madison): "From these facts, by which Montesquieu was guided, it may clearly be inferred that in saying 'There can be no liberty where the legislative and executive powers are united in the same person, or body of magistrates,' or, 'if the power of judging be not separated from the legislative and executive powers,' he did not mean that these departments ought to have no *partial agency* in, or no *control* over, the acts of each other."

28. See generally Jack M. Beermann, *Common Law and Statute Law in Administrative Law*, 63 Admin. L. Rev. 1 (2011).

CHAPTER 2

1. See Robert H. Jackson, *The Federal Prosecutor*, 24 J. Am. Jud. Soc'y 18 (1940).

2. See id.

3. Cass R. Sunstein and Adrian F. Vermeule, *The Law of "Not Now": When Agencies Defer Decisions*, 103 Geo. L.J. 157 (2014).

4. See generally Isaiah Berlin, *Four Essays on Liberty* (1990).

5. See Cass R. Sunstein, *The Second Bill of Rights: FDR's Consititutional Vision and Why We Need It Today* (2025).

6. See Cass R. Sunstein, *Constitutionalism After the New Deal*, 101 Harv. L. Rev. 421 (1987).

7. See Heckler v. Chaney, 470 U.S. 821 (1985); Dunlop v. Bachowski, 421 U.S. 560 (1975).

8. INS v. Chadha, 462 U.S. 919 (1983).

9. Exceptions, of course, are impeachment (in the House) and trial and possibly conviction (in the Senate). See U.S. Const. art. I, §§ 2–3.

10. See Marbury v. Madison, 5 U.S. (1 Cranch) 137, 177 (1803), and in particular these well-known words: "It is emphatically the province and duty of the judicial department to say what the law is."

11. *The Federalist No. 78*, at 466 (Alexander Hamilton) (Clinton Rossiter ed., 2003).

12. There are counterarguments. See Nikolas Bowie and Daphna Renan, *The Separation-of-Powers Counterrevolution*, 131 Yale L.J. 2020, 2095 (2022): "A constitutional discourse based on legal entitlements risks crowding out . . . nonlegal considerations, even in contexts where the legal claim itself is deeply contested, and the moral or policy considerations are especially weighty. It provides a 'limited menu of argument types . . . expected to provide definitive answers' precisely where the goal should be more multifaceted contestation and a more provisional understanding of settlement."

13. James Bradley Thayer, *The Origin and Scope of the American Doctrine of Constitutional Law*, 7 Harv. L. Rev. 129 (1893).

14. Paul Brest, *The Conscientious Legislator's Guide to Constitutional Interpretation*, 27 Stan. L. Rev. 585 (1975).

15. See Ronald Dworkin, *Freedom's Law: The Moral Reading of the American Constitution* (1996).

16. See Antonin Scalia, *Originalism: The Lesser Evil*, 57 U. Cinn. L. Rev. 849, 854 (1989).

17. An argument in favor of judicial superiority can be found in Alexander M. Bickel, *The Least Dangerous Branch: The Supreme Court at the Bar of Politics* (1962); see also Dworkin, supra note 15.

18. See John Hart Ely, *Democracy and Distrust: A Theory of Judicial Review* (1980).

19. See generally Lon L. Fuller, *The Morality of Law* (Yale Univ. Press, rev. ed. 1969) (1964); Joseph Raz, *The Authority of Law: Essays on Law and Morality* (1979); and John

Tasioulas, *The Rule of Law*, in *The Cambridge Companion to the Philosophy of Law* 117 (John Tasioulas ed., 2020).

20. Caleb Nelson, *What Is Textualism?*, 91 Va. L. Rev. 347, 351–357 (2013).

21. Kent v. Dulles, 357 U.S. 116, 128–129 (1958).

22. See, for example, Bowen v. Georgetown Univ. Hosp., 488 U.S. 204, 208 (1988): "Retroactivity is not favored in the law. Thus, congressional enactments and administrative rules will not be construed to have retroactive effect unless their language requires this result."

23. See, for example, EEOC v. Arabian Am. Oil Co., 499 U.S. 244, 248 (1991): "We assume that Congress legislates against the backdrop of the presumption against extraterritoriality. Therefore, unless there is 'the affirmative intention of the Congress clearly expressed,' we must presume it 'is primarily concerned with domestic conditions.'"

24. *The Federalist No. 78*, at 469 (Hamilton).

CHAPTER 3

1. 285 U.S. 22 (1932); see also Commodity Futures Trading Comm'n v. Schor, 478 U.S. 833 (1986).

2. See id. For the best discussion, see Richard H. Fallon Jr., *Of Legislative Courts, Administrative Agencies, and Article III*, 101 Harv. L. Rev. 915 (1988).

3. Youngstown Sheet & Tube Co. v. Sawyer, 343 U.S. 579 (1952).

4. See Cass R. Sunstein, *Going to Extremes: How Like Minds Unite and Divide* (2009).

5. See Jody Freeman and David B. Spence, *Old Statutes, New Problems*, 163 U. Pa. L. Rev. 1 (2014).

6. A.L.A. Schechter Poultry Corp. v. United States, 295 U.S. 495, 539 (1935).

7. Gundy v. United States, 588 U.S. 128, 149 (2019) (Gorsuch, J., dissenting).

8. See Eric A. Posner and Adrian F. Vermeule, *Interring the Nondelegation Doctrine*, 69 U. Chi. L. Rev. 1721 (2002).

9. For a sampling, see, for example, Julian Davis Mortenson and Nicholas Bagley, *Delegation at the Founding*, 121 Colum. L. Rev. 277 (2021); Julian Davis Mortenson and Nicholas Bagley, *Delegation at the Founding: A Response to Critics*, 122 Colum. L. Rev. 2323 (2022); Kevin Arlyck, *Delegation, Administration, and Improvisation*, 97 Notre Dame L. Rev. 243, 248 (2021); Christine Kexel Chabot, *The Lost History of Delegation at the Founding*, 56 Ga. L. Rev. 81, 87–88 (2021); and Nicholas R. Parrillo, *A Critical Assessment of the Originalist Case Against Administrative Regulatory Power: New Evidence from the Federal Tax on Private Real Estate in the 1790s*, 130 Yale L.J. 1288, 1302 (2021).

10. See Cass R. Sunstein, *Epistemic Communities in American Public Law*, 1 Pol. Phil. 181 (2024).

11. See David Epstein and Sharyn O'Halloran, *Delegating Powers: A Transaction Cost Politics Approach to Policy Making Under Separate Powers* (1999).

12. See, for example, Gundy, 588 U.S. at 149 (Gorsuch, J., dissenting).

13. See Cass R. Sunstein, *Nondelegation Canons*, 67 U. Chi. L. Rev. 315 (2000), which appears in revised form as chapter 9 here.

14. See id.

15. Youngstown Sheet & Tube Co. v. Sawyer, 343 U.S. 579 (1952).

16. See H. Jefferson Powell, *The President's Duty to Defend Against Cyber-Attacks*, Harv. L. Rev. Blog (Feb. 22, 2018), https://harvardlawreview.org/blog/2018/02/the-presidents-duty-to-defend-against-cyber-attacks/ [https://perma.cc/8LX6-TP37].

17. See Jules Lobel, *Emergency Power and the Decline of Liberalism*, 98 Yale L.J. 1385 (1989).

18. See Saikrishna Bangalore Prakash, *The Imbecilic Executive*, 99 Va. L. Rev. 1361, 1363–1365 (2013) (articulating various positions over the scope of the executive's emergency powers).

CHAPTER 4

1. This is one way of reading Bi-Metallic Inv. Co. v. State Bd. of Equalization, 239 U.S. 441 (1915). See Kenneth Culp Davis, *An Approach to Problems of Evidence in the Administrative Process*, 55 Harv. L. Rev. 364, 402–403 (1942).

2. Erie R.R. Co. v. Tompkins, 304 U.S. 64 (1937).

3. See David A. Strauss, *The Living Constitution* (2010).

4. For example, you will have noticed that I have not discussed parliamentary systems.

CHAPTER 5

1. Trump v. United States, No. 23-939, slip op. (July 1, 2024).

2. See, for example, Clinton v. Jones, 520 U. S. 681, 692–693 (1997) ("In cases involving prosecutors, legislators, and judges we have repeatedly explained that the immunity serves the public interest in enabling such officials to perform their designated functions effectively without fear that a particular decision may give rise to personal liability"); Nixon v. Fitzgerald, 457 U. S. 731, 751 (1982).

3. The Trump court divides analysis into three categories: (1) absolute immunity, stemming from presidential conduct within conclusive and preclusive authority; (2) presumptive immunity (at least), stemming from presidential conduct within the

outer boundaries of official authority; and (3) no immunity because unofficial acts are involved. My focus here is only on category 1.

4. 343 U.S. 579 (1952); see id. at 635–638 (Jackson, J., concurring).

5. Id. at 637–638.

6. See Trump, slip op. at 9.

7. They are Youngstown, Myers, and Klein, all discussed ahead.

8. Trump, slip op. at 7 (quoting Youngstown Sheet & Steel Tube Co., 343 U.S. at 638) (Jackson, J., concurring).

9. Id.

10. 343 U.S. at 637–638 (Jackson, J., concurring).

11. See Trump, slip op. at 7–8.

12. Id. at 7.

13. Id. at 8.

14. 80 U.S. (13 Wall.) 128 (1871).

15. Id. at 143–144.

16. Id. at 147.

17. See id. at 141: "The President's power of pardon is not subject to legislation; . . . Congress can neither limit the effect of his pardon, nor exclude from its exercise any class of offenders." (Internal quotation marks omitted.)

18. Id. at 148.

19. See id.

20. See Seila Law LLC v. CFPB, 140 S. Ct. 2183, 2109–2200 (2020).

21. Id.

22. Id.

23. See, for example, Clinton v. Jones, 520 U. S. 681 (1997); Nixon v. Fitzgerald, 457 U. S. 731 (1982).

24. A Sitting President's Amenability to Indictment and Crim. Prosecution, 24 Op. OLC 222 (2000). The Trump court appeared to endorse that view, though perhaps it was simply reporting on it. See Trump, slip op. at 10 (quoting Nixon, 457 U.S. at 751, 752, n. 32).

25. Trump, slip op. at 19.

26. Trump, slip op. at 40–41 (emphasis added) (quoting United States v. Johnson, 383 U.S. 169, 172 [1966]).

27. See *The Federalist No. 10* (Madison).

28. I am grateful to Jeannie Suk Gersen for raising this point.

29. See generally John Hart Ely, *Democracy and Distrust* (1980).

30. Id. at 87–88, 135–136.

31. For the American version, see *The Federalist No. 10* (Madison).

32. 531 U.S. 98 (2000).

33. No. 23–719, slip op. (2024).

34. Id. at 11–12.

35. Dred Scott v. Sandford, 60 U.S. (19 How.) 393 (1857), can of course be understood in similar terms.

CHAPTER 8

1. SEC v. Jarkesy, 144 S. Ct. 2117, 2139 (2024).

2. FTC v. Ruberoid Co., 343 U.S. 470, 487 (1952) (Jackson, J., dissenting).

3. For various versions, see Christopher DeMuth, *Can the Administrative State Be Tamed?*, 8 J. Legal Analysis 121 (2016); Jennifer L. Selin, *The Headless Fourth Branch*, 4 Persps. on Pub. Mgmt. and Governance 170 (2021); Philip Hamburger, *Is Administrative Law Unlawful?* (2014); Gary Lawson, *The Rise and Rise of the Administrative State*, 107 Harv. L. Rev. 1231 (1994); and Richard A. Epstein, *The Dubious Morality of Administrative Law* (2020). For discussion of relevant issues, engaging with something like the Grand Narrative, see Cass R. Sunstein, *Constitutionalism After the New Deal*, 101 Harv. L. Rev. 421 (1987); and James Friedman, *Crisis and Legitimacy* (1980).

4. For a vivid account, see DeMuth, supra note 3.

5. See, for example, Ilan Wurman, *Nondelegation at the Founding*, 130 Yale L.J. 1288 (2021); Gary Lawson, *Delegation and Original Meaning*, 88 Va. L. Rev. 327 (2002); Philip Hamburger, *Nondelegation Blues*, 91 Geo. Wash. L. Rev. (2023); Richard A. Epstein, *Delegation of Powers: A Historical and Functional Analysis*, 24 Chap. L. Rev. 659 (2021); Aaron Gordon, *Nondelegation Misinformation: A Reply to the Skeptics*, 75 Baylor L. Rev. 152 (2023); and Hamburger, supra note 3.

6. David Schoenbrod, *Power Without Responsibility: How Congress Abuses the People Through Delegation* (1993).

7. A.L.A. Schechter Poultry Corp. v. United States, 295 U.S. 495 (1935).

8. See Hamburger, supra note 3.

9. Aditya Bamzai and Saikrishna Bangalore Prakash, *The Executive Power of Removal*, 136 Harv. L. Rev. 1758 (2023); Saikrishna Prakash, *New Light on the Decision of 1789*, 91 Cornell. L. Rev. 1021 (2006).

10. See Bijal Shah, *Congress's Agency Coordination*, 103 Minn. L. Rev. 1961, 2033 n.332 (2019) ("[The] headless 'fourth branch' of government consists of independent agencies having significant duties in both the legislative and executive branches but

residing not entirely within either" [alteration in original] [quoting Ameron, Inc. v. U.S. Army Corps of Eng'rs, 787 F.2d 875, 886 (3d Cir. 1986)]); Arlington v. FCC, 569 U.S. 290, 314 (2013) (Roberts, C.J., dissenting) ("The collection of agencies housed outside the traditional executive departments . . . is routinely described as the 'headless fourth branch of government,' reflecting not only the scope of their authority but their practical independence."). See also FTC v. Ruberoid Co., 343 U.S. 470, 487 (1952) (Jackson, J., dissenting), referring to "a veritable fourth branch of the Government, which has deranged our three-branch legal theories."

11. U.S. Const. art III, § 1.

12. Id.

13. See, for example, Harold Krent, *Presidential Control of Adjudication Within the Executive Branch*, 65 Case Wes. Res. L. Rev. 1083 (2015).

14. See Richard Epstein, *How Progressives Rewrote the Constitution* (2006).

15. Hamburger, supra note 3.

16. See Philip Hamburger, *Chevron Bias*, 84 G.W. L. Rev. 1187 (2016). It might be noted parenthetically that Chief Justice Roberts tends to write opinions with distinctive narratives of the arc of the law; he is exceptionally skilled at it. See, for example, Seila Law LLC. v. CFPB, 591 U.S. 197 (2020); and Loper Bright Enters. v. Raimondo, 144 S. Ct. 2244 (2024).

17. Here are three: Richard Stewart, *The Reformation of American Administrative Law*, 88 Harv. L. Rev. 1667 (1975); Jerry Mashaw, *Reasoned Administration and Democratic Legitimacy* (2018); and Cass R. Sunstein and Adrian Vermeule, *Law and Leviathan* (2020). As they say, the owl of Minerva flies only at dusk. Maybe it is dusk. We should hope so. For a night-flying owl, see John Hart Ely, *Democracy and Distrust* (1980).

18. See Gundy v. United States, 588 U.S. 128 (2019) (Gorsuch, J., dissenting).

19. 295 U.S. 602 (1935).

20. Wiener v. United States, 357 U.S. 349 (1958).

21. 285 U.S. 22 (1932). The best discussion remains Richard H. Fallon, *Of Legislative Courts, Administrative Agencies, and Article III*, 101 Harv. L. Rev. 915 (1988).

22. Northern Pipeline Constr. Co. v. Marathon Pipe Line Co., 458 U.S. 50 (1982); and Thomas v. Union Carbide Agric. Products Co., 473 U.S. 568 (1985). The Seventh Amendment analogue, a clear target of the Grand Narrative, is Atlas Roofing Co. v. Occupational Safety and Health Review Comm'n, 430 U.S. 442 (1977).

23. See, for example, Touby v. United States, 500 U.S. 160 (1991); and Industrial Union Department, AFL-CIO v. American Petroleum Institute, 448 U.S. 607 (1980).

24. Whitman v. American Trucking Ass'ns., Inc., 531 U.S. 457 (2001).

25. Id.

26. Id. at 474 (internal citations omitted).

27. See Bowsher v. Synar, 478 U.S. 714, 725–726 (1986).

28. See, for example, Northern Pipeline Constr. Co. v. Marathon Pipe Line Co., 458 U.S. 50 (1982); Thomas v. Union Carbide Agric. Products Co., 473 U.S. 568 (1985); and Stern v. Marshall, 564 U.S. 462 (2011).

29. See Randy Barnett, *Restoring the Lost Constitution* (2013).

30. Free Enter. Fund v. Pub. Co. Acct. Oversight Bd., 561 U.S. 477 (2010).

31. Id. at 483.

32. Id.

33. Id. at 484.

34. Seila Law LLC v. CFPB, 591 U.S. 197 (2020).

35. Id. at 203–204.

36. See Aditya Bamzai and Saikrishna Bangalore Prakash, *The Executive Power of Removal*, 136 Harv. L. Rev. 1758 (2023); Saikrishna Prakash, *New Light on the Decision of 1789*, 91 Cornell. L. Rev. 1021 (2006).

37. Seila Law LLC v. CFPB, 591 U.S. 197, 218 (2020).

38. Id.

39. Humphrey's Executor v. United States, 295 U.S. 602, 628 (1935): "Under § 7, which authorizes the commission to act as a master in chancery under rules prescribed by the court, it acts as an agency of the judiciary." Id. at 628.

40. "In making investigations and reports thereon for the information of Congress under 6, in aid of the legislative power, it acts as a legislative agency." Id.

41. See Nat'l Petroleum Refiners Ass'n. v. FTC, 482 F.2d 672 (D.C. Cir. 1973).

42. Humphrey's Executor v. United States, 295 U.S. 602, 628 (1935) ("The Federal Trade Commission is an administrative body created by Congress to carry into effect legislative policies embodied in the statute in accordance with the legislative standard therein prescribed, and to perform other specified duties as a legislative or as a judicial aid. Such a body cannot in any proper sense be characterized as an arm or an eye of the executive.").

43. See Geoffrey Miller, *Independent Agencies*, 1986 Sup. Ct. Rev. 41 (1986).

44. Wiener v. United States, 357 U.S. 349 (1958).

45. 467 U.S. 837 (1984).

46. See Loper Bright Enters. v. Raimondo, 144 S. Ct. 2244, 2289 (2024) (Gorsuch, J., concurring).

47. 5 U.S.C. 706.

48. Loper Bright Enters. v. Raimondo, 144 S. Ct. 2244, 2257 (2024) (internal citations omitted).

49. Id.

50. Crowell v. Benson, 285 U.S. 22 (1932).

51. Id. at 51.

52. Id. at 50.

53. Northern Pipeline Constr. Co. v. Marathon Pipe Line Co., 458 U.S. 50 (1982); and Thomas v. Union Carbide Agric. Products Co., 473 U.S. 568 (1985).

54. SEC v. Jarkesy, 144 S. Ct. 2117, 2133 (2024) (internal citations omitted).

55. Id. at 2148 (Gorsuch, J., concurring).

56. Id.

57. 588 U.S. 128 (2019).

58. Id.

59. Id. (Gorsuch, J., dissenting).

60. Id. at 155–156.

61. Id. at 163–164.

62. Id. at 148–149.

63. West Virginia v. EPA, 597 U.S. 697 (2022).

64. Id. at 723.

65. Id. at 736–753 (Gorsuch, J., concurring).

66. Id. at 740.

67. Id. at 742 (quoting Amy Coney Barrett, *Substantive Canons and Faithful Agency*, 90 B.U. L. Rev. 109, 175 [2010]).

68. Or in the terms of Star Wars, *A New Hope*.

69. *The Empire Strikes Back*.

70. *The Return of the Jedi* (as if you needed to be told).

71. See Dep't of Homeland Security v. Regents of UC, 591 U.S. 1 (2020). There is an unmistakable trend in the direction of aggressive judicial review of agency action, fueled (I think) by the Grand Narrative. See Donald Goodson et al., *Major Rules in the Courts* (2024), available at https://papers.ssrn.com/sol3/papers.cfm?abstract_id =4819477.

72. See Julian Davis Mortenson and Nicholas Bagley, *Delegation at the Founding*, 121 Colum. L. Rev. 277 (2021). I count myself as part of Camp Burkeanism and Camp Pragmatism, but I only sketch, and do not defend, my view here.

73. Id. Mortenson and Bagley offer a vivid argument that it does not, at least insofar as we are speaking of the nondelegation doctrine.

74. I am bracketing some questions about how to identify the original public meaning. For defining discussions, see Lawrence Solum, *Originalist Methodology*, 84 U. Chi. L. Rev. 269 (2017); and Lawrence B. Solum, *Triangulating Public Meaning: Corpus Linguistics, Immersion, and the Constitutional Record*, 2017 BYU L. Rev. 1621 (2017)

75. See Mortenson and Bagley, supra note 73; Eric Posner and Adrian F. Vermeule, *Interring the Nondelegation Doctrine*, 69 U. Chi. L. Rev. 1721 (2002); Nicholas R. Parrillo, *A Critical Assessment of the Originalist Case Against Administrative Regulatory Power: New Evidence from the Federal Tax on Private Real Estate in the 1790s*, 130 Yale L.J. 1288 (2021); and Christine Kexel Chabot, *The Lost History of Delegation at the Founding*, 56 Ga. L. Rev. 81 (2021).

76. See Keith Whittington and Jason Iuliano, *The Myth of The Nondelegation Doctrine*, 165 U. Pa. L. Rev. 379 (2017); Jerry L. Mashaw, *Creating the Administrative Constitution: The Lost One Hundred Years of American Administrative Law* 5 (2012) ("From the earliest days of the Republic, Congress delegated broad authority to administrators, armed them with extrajudicial coercive powers, created systems of administrative adjudication, and specifically authorized administrative rulemaking.").

77. See *The Invention of Tradition* (Eric Hobsbawm and Terrence Ranger eds. 1992).

78. Maurice Halbwachs, *On Collective Memory* 234 (1992).

79. Julian Davis Mortenson and Nicholas Bagley, *Delegation at the Founding: A Response to Critics*, 122 Colum. L. Rev. 2323 (2022); Kevin Arlyck, *Delegation, Administration, and Improvisation*, 97 Notre Dame L. Rev. 243, 248 (2021); Chabot, supra note 76, at 87–88; and Whittington and Iuliano, supra note 76.

80. This is a plausible reading of Mortenson and Bagley, supra note 72; Mortenson and Bagley, supra note 79.

81. To be sure, there is a question here about the right conception of originalism; I will turn to that question ahead.

82. Jed H. Shugerman, *The Indecisions of 1789: Inconstant Originalism and Strategic Ambiguity*, 171 U Pa. L. Rev. 753 (2023); Mashaw, *Creating the Administrative Constitution* (2012); Jed H. Shugerman, *Removal of Context: Blackstone, Limited Monarchy, and the Limits of Unitary Originalism*, 33 Yale J.L. & Humans. (2022); and Jed H. Shugerman, *Vesting*, 74 Stan. L. Rev. 1479 (2022).

83. Jed H. Shugerman, *The Indecisions of 1789: Inconstant Originalism and Strategic Ambiguity*, 171 U Pa. L. Rev. 753 (2023), strongly supports the view that the majority in Congress did not believe that the Constitution granted the president plenary removal authority.

84. See Jerry L. Mashaw, *Recovering American Administrative Law: Federalist Foundations, 1787–1801*, 115 Yale L.J. 1256 (2006).

85. See Cass R. Sunstein, *How to Interpret the Constitution* (2023).

86. On Burkeanism, see Cass R. Sunstein, *Burkean Minimalism*, 105 Mich. L. Rev. 253 (2006).

87. Edmund Burke, *Reflections on the Revolution in France*, in *The Portable Edmund Burke* 416, 456–457 (Isaac Kramnick ed., 1999).

88. Id. (emphasis added).

89. Gundy v. United States, 588 U.S. 128, 149 (2019)

90. See James Bradley Thayer, *The Origin and Scope of the American Doctrine of Constitutional Law*, 7 Harv. L. Rev. 129 (1893). For a valuable discussion of Thayer's motivations, emphasizing what he sees as Thayer's political conservatism and desire to activate political focus on combating ill-considered progressivism, see generally Mark Tushnet, *Thayer's Target: Judicial Review or Democracy?*, 88 Nw. U. L. Rev. 9 (1993).

91. Thayer, supra note 90, at 135.

92. See id. at 140 (quoting Com. v. Smith, 4 Bin 117 [1811]) (emphasis added). Note that this claim is not the same as the "rational basis" test for reviewing legislation. The rational basis test is rooted in *the court's independent interpretation* of the requirements of various constitutional provisions—in the court's view, what is required is a rational basis (no more and no less). The court does not say that it adopts the rational basis test because in Congress's view of the Constitution, that test is the right one.

93. Thayer, supra note 90, at 140.

94. Id. at 141.

95. Id. at 144.

96. The obligatory citation, and the right one, is McCulloch v. Maryland, 17 U.S. 316 (1819)—and, of course:

> In considering this question, then, we must never forget that it is *a Constitution* we are expounding. . . . The subject is the execution of those great powers on which the welfare of a Nation essentially depends. It must have been the intention of those who gave these powers to insure, so far as human prudence could insure, their beneficial execution. This could not be done by confiding the choice of means to such narrow limits as not to leave it in the power of Congress to adopt any which might be appropriate, and which were conducive to the end. This provision is made in a Constitution intended to endure for ages to come, and consequently to be adapted to the various crises of human affairs. To have prescribed the means by which Government should, in all future time, execute its powers would have been to change entirely the character of the instrument and give it the properties of a legal code. It would have been an unwise attempt to provide by immutable rules for exigencies which, if foreseen at all, must have been seen dimly, and which can be best provided for as they occur.

97. David Epstein and Sharyn O'Halloran, *Delegating Powers* (1999).

98. For different accounts, see Eric MacGilvray, *Liberal Freedom, the Separation of Powers, and the Administrative State*, 38 Soc. Phil. and Pol'y. 120 (2021); Jerry Mashaw, *Prodelegation: Why Administrators Should Make Political Decisions*, 1 J.L., Econ., and

Org. 81 (1985); Cass R. Sunstein, *The Cost-Benefit Revolution* (2018); and Epstein and O'Halloran, supra note 98.

CHAPTER 9

1. See, for example, Bowen v. Georgetown University Hospital, 488 US 204, 208–209 (1988) (stating that a congressional delegation of authority will be understood as granting the power to make retroactive rules only if the Congress specifically said so).

2. See, for example, Muscogee (Creek) Nation v. Hodel, 851 F2d 1439, 1444–1445 (DC Cir 1988) (stating that "canons of construction applicable in Indian law" require that "statutes are to be construed liberally in favor of the Indians, with ambiguous provisions interpreted to their benefit").

3. See Rust v. Sullivan, 500 US 173, 191 (1991).

4. See id.

5. See National Association of Regulatory Utility Commissioners v. FCC, 880 F2d 422 (DC Cir 1989).

6. See Herbert Wechsler, *The Political Safeguards of Federalism*, 54 Colum. L. Rev. 543 (1954), for the classic discussion of these safeguards.

7. It is not entirely clear whether an agency might be able to answer the question if Congress expressly said that the agency is permitted to do so. This raises a general point about the nondelegation canons: What would happen if Congress attempted to bypass them by a clear statement of delegation?

8. Bowen v. Georgetown University Hospital, 488 US 204, 208 (1988).

9. Id.

10. The notion is defended in Richard A. Epstein, *Takings: Private Property and the Power of Eminent Domain* 255–259 (Harvard 1985).

11. See, for example, Usery v. Turner Elkhorn Mining, 438 US 1, 14–20 (1976) (holding that the Black Lung Benefits Act of 1972 does not violate the Fifth Amendment Due Process Clause by requiring employers to provide retrospective compensation for former employees' death or disability due to employment in mines).

12. EEOC v. Arabian American Oil Co, 499 US 244, 248 (1991).

13. Of course, the executive is permitted to make many quite sensitive decisions involving foreign relations—partly because of express constitutional commitments, partly because of perceived contemporary necessities. And it would not be impossible to imagine a legal system in which the executive was permitted, in the event of ambiguity, to resolve the issue of extraterritoriality. Recall that my goal here is descriptive, not normative. The best defense of this particular nondelegation canon would be that the question whether the enacted law should be applied outside of

144
the nation's borders is a large and essentially legislative one, which cannot be made by the executive on its own.

14. See Ramah Navajo Chapter v. Lujan, 112 F3d 1455, 1461–1462 (10th Cir 1997) (grounding a canon of statutory construction favoring Native Americans in "the unique trust relationship between the United States and the Indians"); Williams v. Babbitt, 115 F2d 657, 660 (9th Cir 1997) (noting in dicta that courts "are required to construe statutes favoring Native Americans liberally in their favor"); and Tyonek Native Corp v. Secretary of Interior, 836 F2d 1237, 1239 (9th Cir 1988) (noting in dicta that "statutes benefiting Native Americans should be construed liberally in their favor").

15. United States Department of Energy v. Ohio, 503 US 607, 615 (1992).

16. United States v. Wells Fargo Bank, 485 US 351, 354 (1988).

17. Michigan Citizens for an Independent Press v. Thornburgh, 868 F2d 1285, 1299 (DC Cir 1989) (Ginsburg, J., dissenting) (noting the "accepted rule" that antitrust exemptions must be narrowly construed); and Group Life & Health Insurance v. Royal Drug Co, 440 US 205, 231 (1979) (noting the "well settled" rule that antitrust exceptions "are to be narrowly construed").

18. King v. St. Vincent's Hospital, 502 US 215, 220n9 (1991).

19. See Industrial Union Department, AFL-CIO v. American Petroleum Institute, 448 US 607, 644 (1980) (plurality) (holding that in enacting OSHA, Congress "intended, at a bare minimum, that the Secretary [of Labor] find a significant risk of harm and therefore a probability of significant benefits before establishing a new standard"); Corrosion Proof Fittings v. EPA, 947 F2d 1201, 1222–23 (5th Cir. 1991) (vacating the EPA's proposed rulemaking under the Toxic Substances Control Act and its ban on asbestos, partially on the grounds that the agency's own figures suggested that enforcing the regulation might cost as much as $74 million per life saved); Alabama Power Co v. Costle, 636 F2d 323, 360–361 (DC Cir 1979) (stating that "[u]nless Congress has been extraordinarily rigid, there is likely a basis for an implication of de minimis authority to provide exemption when the burdens of regulation yield a gain of trivial or no value"); and Monsanto Co. v. Kennedy, 613 F2d 947, 954–955 (DC Cir 1979) (allowing the Commissioner of Food and Drugs not to apply the strictly literal terms of the statute and to make de minimis exceptions).

20. See Richard A. Posner, *The Federal Courts: Challenge and Reform* 285 (2d rev. ed. 1999).

CHAPTER 10

1. FDA v. Brown & Williamson Tobacco Corp., 529 U.S. 120, 159–160 (2000), superseded by statute, Family Smoking Prevention and Tobacco Control Act, Pub. L. No. 111–131, 123 Stat. 1776 (2009) (codified at 21 U.S.C. § 387).

2. Biden v. Nebraska, 143 S. Ct. 2355, 2373 (2023).

3. West Virginia v. EPA, 142 S. Ct. 2587, 2608 (2022).

4. See generally Cass R. Sunstein, *There Are Two "Major Questions" Doctrines*, 73 Ad. L. Rev. 475 (2021).

5. See Gundy v. United States, 139 S. Ct. 2116, 2133–2134 (2019) (Gorsuch, J., dissenting).

6. John Locke, *Two Treatises on Civil Government* § 141 (George Routledge & Sons ed., Ballantone Press 1884) (1689); see also Gundy, 139 S. Ct. at 2133–2134 (quoting Locke). Note, however, that the meaning of Locke's words is disputed; it is not at all clear that he had anything like the modern American nondelegation doctrine in mind. See Julian Davis Mortenson and Nicholas Bagley, *Delegation at the Founding*, 121 Colum. L. Rev. 277, 307–308 (2021). I am (mostly) bracketing here the constitutional foundations of that doctrine.

7. West Virginia, 142 S. Ct. at 2616 (Gorsuch, J., concurring).

8. I am bracketing the difficulty of deciding what makes a question "major," or what makes an interpretation "extraordinary." Justice Gorsuch has attempted to offer a framework to answer that question. See West Virginia, 142 S. Ct. at 2620–2622.

9. See Biden v. Nebraska, 143 S. Ct. 2355, 2379–2380 (2023) (Barrett, J., concurring).

10. For a similar account, see Ilan Wurman, *Importance and Interpretive Questions*, 110 Virginia L. Rev. 909 (2024). Wurman draws on the highly instructive analysis in Ryan D. Doerfler, *High-Stakes Interpretation*, 116 Mich. L. Rev. 523, 527 (2018).

11. Ludwig Wittgenstein, *Philosophical Investigations* 33 (G. E. M. Anscombe trans., 3d ed. 1967).

12. Biden, 143 S. Ct. at 2379.

13. See id. at 2380.

14. Id.

15. Id. (quoting Util. Air Regul. Grp. v. EPA, 573 U.S. 302, 324 [2014]).

16. Id. (quoting U.S. Telecom Ass'n v. FCC, 855 F.3d 381, 419 [D.C. Cir. 2017] [Kavanaugh, J., dissenting from denial of reh'g en banc]).

17. Id. This view is not simple to defend as a matter of history. See Mortenson and Bagley, supra note 6, at 331–332; Jerry Mashaw, *Creating the Administrative Constitution: The Lost One Hundred Years of American Administrative Law* 291 (2012). The terms *big time* and *pawning off* do not fit well with long-standing practice. From the earliest days of the Republic, Congress granted broad discretion to executive authorities. See Mashaw, supra at 33; Mortensen and Bagley, supra note 6, at 332–349.

18. Biden, 143 S. Ct. at 2381.

19. Id. at 2377–2378.

20. Id. at 2381.

21. Id. at 2376.

22. See id. at 2376. In my view, she is too cautious about them. See Cass R. Sunstein, *Interpreting Statutes in the Regulatory State*, 103 Harv. L. Rev. 405, 504 (1989) (arguing that canons of construction "must occupy a prominent place in the theory and practice of statutory interpretation"). I should add that the present author does not agree with everything said by the young author of id.

23. Biden, 143 S. Ct. at 2376.

24. See id.

25. Id. at 2376–2377.

26. Id. (quoting Amy Coney Barrett, *Substantive Canons and Faithful Agency*, 90 B.U. L. Rev. 109, 123–124 [2010]).

27. Id. at 2377 n.2.

28. MCI Telecomms. Corp. v. Am. Tel. & Tel. Corp., 512 U.S. 218, 225 (1994), superseded by statute, Telecomms. Act of 1996, Pub. L. No. 104–104, 110 Stat. 128 (codified at 47 U.S.C. § 160[a][1]).

29. Biden, 143 S. Ct. at 224–225 (quoting 47 U.S.C. § 203[b][2]).

30. Id. at 231.

31. Id.

32. Wurman, supra note 10 (offering a sharp criticism of MCI when the opinion is taken purely as a textualist opinion).

33. MCI Telecomms. Corp., 512 U.S. at 225.

34. Id. at 228.

35. Id. at 231.

36. Id. at 231–232.

37. Id. at 232.

38. See, for example, Biden at 2369.

39. Although I will not explore the point here, there is an uncomfortable relationship between the major questions doctrine as understood by Justice Gorsuch and the old, discredited idea that "statutes in derogation of the common law will be narrowly construed." See generally Jefferson B. Fordham and J. Russell Leach, *Interpretation of Statutes in Derogation of the Common Law*, 3 Vand. L. Rev. 438 (1950) (providing a historical understanding of the derogation canon). We could easily understand some versions of the major questions doctrine to fall in the same category as constitutional and statutory decisions of the Lochner era. I am keenly aware that Justice Gorsuch would reject this suggestion and that I have not defended it here.

40. Biden, 143 S. Ct. at 2380 (Barrett, J., concurring).

41. Justice Kagan offered a powerful and maybe even devastating response; see Biden, 143 S. Ct. at 2397 (Kagan, J., dissenting):

> Here is a fact of the matter: Congress delegates to agencies often and broadly. And it usually does so for sound reasons. Because agencies have expertise Congress lacks. Because times and circumstances change, and agencies are better able to keep up and respond. Because Congress knows that if it had to do everything, many desirable and even necessary things wouldn't get done. In wielding the major-questions sword, last Term and this one, this Court overrules those legislative judgments. The doctrine forces Congress to delegate in highly specific terms—respecting, say, loan forgiveness of certain amounts for borrowers of certain incomes during pandemics of certain magnitudes. Of course Congress sometimes delegates in that way. But also often not.

42. Pub. L. No. 159–360, 69 Stat. 322 (1955) (codified as amended at 42 U.S.C. §§ 7401–7671).

43. 42 U.S.C. § 7409(b)(1).

44. Pub. L. No. 89–563, 80 Stat. 718 (1966) (codified as amended at 49 U.S.C. § 30111).

45. 49 U.S.C. § 30111(a).

46. Cameron Gulbransen Kids Transportation Safety Act of 2007, Pub. L. No. 110–189, § 2(b) (2008) (codified at 49 U.S.C. § 30111 note).

47. See Cass R. Sunstein, *Rear Visibility and Some Unresolved Problems for Cost-Benefit Analysis*, 10 J Benefit-Cost Analysis 317 (2019).

48. 49 U.S.C. § 30111 note.

49. See Mortensen and Bagley, supra note 6, at 332–349 (providing a long list of examples from the early Republic).

50. I once testified before a congressional committee and suggested that Congress should introduce greater uniformity by specifying the figure. Members looked at me as if I had lost my mind. (Maybe I had.)

51. See Wittgenstein, supra note 13, at 48.

`52. See West Virginia v. EPA, 142 S. Ct. 2587, 2616 (2022) (Gorsuch, J., concurring).

53. See David S. Romantic, *Reconstructing the Rule of Lenity*, 40 Cardozo L. Rev. 523, 524 (2018).

54. See Murray v. Schooner Charming Betsy, 6 U.S. (2 Cranch) 64, 118 (1804).

55. See West Virginia, 142 S. Ct. at 2616–2617.

56. See Mortenson and Bagley, supra note 6, at 331–349.

57. See Church of the Holy Trinity v. United States, 143 U.S. 457, 460 (1892).

58. John F. Manning, *The Absurdity Doctrine*, 116 Harv. L. Rev. 2387, 2388–2389 (2003).

59. Michigan v. EPA, 576 U.S. 743, 750–751 (2015).

60. That idea helps explain *Kent v. Dulles*, 357 U.S. 116, 129 (1958), which could be seen as an early use of something like the major questions doctrine—though it is (in my view) best taken as a simple application of the Avoidance Canon.

61. See Env't Def. Fund v. Ruckelshaus, 439 F.2d 584, 592–594 (D.C. Cir. 1971) (requiring the EPA to regulate DDT).

62. The doctrine is sometimes traced to Industrial Union Department, AFL-CIO v. American Petroleum Institute, 448 U.S. 607, 645 (1980) (plurality opinion). The connection is not impossible to defend, but the plurality opinion is better taken to reflect the Avoidance Canon and the Absurdity Canon.

63. West Virginia v. EPA, 142 S. Ct. 2587, 2610 (2022).

64. FDA v. Brown & Williamson Tobacco Corp., 529 U.S. 120, 130 (2000), superseded by statute, Family Smoking Prevention and Tobacco Control Act, Pub. L. No. 111–131, 123 Stat. 1776 (2009) (codified at 21 U.S.C. § 387).

65. MCI Telecomms. Corp. v. Am. Tel. & Tel. Corp., 512 U.S. 218, 225 (1994), superseded by statute, Telecomms. Act of 1996, Pub. L. No. 104–104, 110 Stat. 128 (codified at 47 U.S.C. § 160[a][1]).

66. MCI Telecomms. Corp., 512 U.S. at 225; Biden v. Nebraska, 143 S. Ct. 2355, 2368 (2023).

67. West Virginia, 142 S. Ct. at 2615–2616.

68. Id. at 2617–2618 (Gorsuch, J., concurring).

69. Biden, 143 S. Ct. at 2380 (Barrett, J., concurring).

70. See Cass R. Sunstein, *Incompletely Theorized Agreements*, 108 Harv. L. Rev. 1733, 1735–1736 (1995).

71. See West Virginia, 142 S. Ct. at 2609 (majority opinion) ("Thus, in certain extraordinary cases, both separation of powers principles and a practical understanding of legislative intent make us 'reluctant to read into ambiguous statutory text' the delegation claimed to be lurking there. To convince us otherwise, something more than a merely plausible textual basis for the agency action is necessary. The agency instead must point to 'clear congressional authorization' for the power it claims."). This statement refers to both the Lockean ("separation of powers") and the Wittgensteinian ("a practical understanding of legislative intent") justifications. Id.; see also Indus. Union Dep't v. Am. Petroleum Inst., 448 U.S. 607, 646 (1980) (plurality opinion) (invoking the canon of constitutional avoidance). By contrast, *Alabama Association of Realtors v. Department of Health & Human Services*, 141 S. Ct. 2485 (2021), can be understood to fit with Justice Barrett's position: "We expect Congress to speak clearly when authorizing an agency to exercise powers of 'vast economic and political significance.' . . . That is exactly the kind of power that the CDC claims here." Supra at 2489. This statement does not reject Justice Gorsuch's

view, but it could be taken to channel Wittgenstein on games. *National Federation of Independent Business v. OSHA*, 142 S. Ct. 661, 667 (2022) (Gorsuch, J., concurring) can be similarly taken.

CHAPTER 11

1. See James Bradley Thayer, *The Origin and Scope of the American Doctrine of Constitutional Law*, 7 Harv. L. Rev. 129 (1893). For a valuable discussion of Thayer's motivations, emphasizing what he sees as Thayer's political conservatism and desire to activate political focus on combating ill-considered progressivism, see generally Mark Tushnet, *Thayer's Target: Judicial Review or Democracy?*, 88 Nw. U. L. Rev. 9 (1993).

2. See Thayer, supra note 1, at 129.

3. *Holmes-Laski Letters: The Correspondence of Mr. Justice Holmes and Harold J. Laski 1916–1935* 249 (Mark DeWolfe Howe ed., 1953).

4. Thayer, supra note 1, at 129.

5. Id. at 130.

6. 5 U.S. 137 (1803).

7. Thayer, supra note 1, at 130.

8. Id. at 131.

9. Id.

10. Id. at 132.

11. Id. at 135.

12. Id.

13. Id. at 136.

14. Id. at 138.

15. Id.

16. See id. at 140 (quoting Com. v. Smith, 4 Bin 117 [1811]) (emphasis added).

17. Thayer, supra note 1, at 140.

18. Id. at 141.

19. Id. at 144.

20. Id.

21. Id. at 149.

22. Id. at 148.

23. Id. at 155.

24. Id. at 147.

25. 198 U.S. 45 (1905).

26. 347 U.S. 497 (1954).

27. 558 U.S. 310 (2010).

28. Thayer, supra note 1, at 150.

29. Id. at 143.

30. Id. at 155.

31. Id. at 156.

32. Id.

33. Learned Hand, *Liberty Lies in the Hearts of Men and Women* (1944), reprinted in *Our Nation's Archives: The History of the United States in Documents* 658 (Erik Bruun and Jay Crosby eds., 1999).

34. Brad Snyder, *Democratic Justice: Felix Frankfurter, the Supreme Court, and the Makings of the Liberal Establishment* 21 (2022).

35. Id.

36. Thayer, supra note 1, at 154.

37. Id. at 155.

38. Jud Campbell, *Natural Rights and the First Amendment*, 127 Yale L.J. 246, 263 (2017).

39. Note, *Blasphemy Laws and the Original Meaning of the First Amendment*, 135 Harv. L. Rev. 689, 691 (2021).

40. Max Crema and Lawrence Solum, *The Original Meaning of "Due Process of Law" in the Fifth Amendment*, 108 Va. L. Rev. 447 (2022).

41. See generally Ronald Dworkin, *Freedom's Law: The Moral Reading of the American Constitution* (1997).

42. See generally Adrian Vermeule, *Common Good Constitutionalism* (2022).

43. See generally Alexander M. Bickel, *The Least Dangerous Branch: The Supreme Court at the Bar of Politics* (1962).

44. See generally Cass R. Sunstein, *One Case at a Time: Judicial Minimalism on the Supreme Court* (1999).

45. See Bickel, supra note 43.

46. Id. at 35.

47. See Lochner v. New York, 198 U.S. 45, 75 (1905) (Holmes, J., dissenting); Adkins v. Children's Hospital, 261 U.S. 525, 568 (1923) (Holmes, J., dissenting); Coppage v. Kansas, 236 U.S. 1, 27 (1915) (Holmes, J., dissenting).

48. Lochner, 198 U.S. at 75 (Holmes, J., dissenting).

49. Buck v. Bell, 274 U.S. 200, 207 (1927).

50. See Abrams v. United States, 250 U.S. 616, 624 (1919) (Holmes, J., dissenting).

51. See Thomas Healy, *The Great Dissent: How Oliver Wendell Holmes Changed His Mind—and Changed the History of Free Speech in America* (2013).

52. See Snyder, supra note 34.

53. This is one reading of Snyder, supra note 34.

54. See, for example, id., at 406–429.

55. 347 U.S. 483 (1954).

56. 347 U.S. 497 (1954).

57. See Snyder, supra note 34, at 430–457.

58. See id.

59. Id. at 406–429. A key example is Justice Frankfurter's dissenting opinion in West Virginia State Board of Education v. Barnette, 319 U.S. 624 (1943).

60. See W. Coast Hotel Co. v. Parrish, 300 U.S. 379 (1937); see also Williamson v. Lee Optical Co., 348 U.S. 483 (1955).

61. See W. Coast Hotel Co., 300 U.S. 379; see also Williamson, 348 U.S. 483.

62. Some of the tale is told illuminatingly in Snyder, supra note 34.

63. Bickel, supra note 43, at 37.

64. Id.

65. Id. at 39.

66. Id.

67. Id.

68. Bickel, supra note 43, at 42.

69. Id. at 42–43.

70. Id. at 45.

71. Id. at 26.

72. Id.

73. Bickel's general approach was, in my view, a clear precursor of Dworkin's. See Ronald Dworkin, *The Forum of Principle*, 56 N.Y.U. L Rev. 469, 516 (1981).

74. John Hart Ely, *Democracy and Distrust: A Theory of Judicial Review*, dedication page (1980).

75. 304 U.S. 144 (1938).

76. Id. at 152 n.4 (1938).

77. See Ely, supra note 74; see generally Stephen Breyer, *Active Liberty: Interpreting Our Democratic Constitution* (2006).

78. Astonishingly? No.

79. For some clues about why contemporary originalists might abhor Thayerism, see Steven G. Calabresi, *Originalism and James Bradley Thayer*, 113 Nw. L. Rev. 1419 (2019). With the reader's indulgence, consider this, supra at 1423, 1454:

> It is important, in evaluating Professor Thayer, to keep in mind that he was a Progressive Era intellectual who, like most Progressives in the 1890s, probably disfavored the Madisonian system of checks and balances, the original meaning of our written Constitution and Bill of Rights, and judicial review, and who probably favored responsible parliamentary government, which then prevailed in the United Kingdom and which Woodrow Wilson alleged to have been "shown" superior to the American system. Woodrow Wilson was an impractical intellectual who would go on to serve as President of Princeton University, Governor of New Jersey, and, for two terms, President of the United States. Like Wilson, Professor Thayer probably thought the Constitution, as originally designed, was a disguised structure for helping the rich to rob the poor. . . .
>
> This ignorance [of the world of the 1890s] led to European colonialism, Jim Crow segregation in the United States, the eugenics movement in the United States and in Germany, the rise of the expert, undemocratic agency, and finally, the move from eugenics to the Holocaust in Germany.

No comment, really, except that there appears to be no evidence in support of these claims about what Thayer "probably" thought (and you can be a progressive, even of the 1890s variety, without hoping for Jim Crow segregation or the Holocaust). For a valuable discussion, see G. Edward White, *Revisiting James Bradley Thayer*, 88 Nw. L. Rev. 48 (1993).

80. See generally Lino Graglia, *Courting Disaster: The Supreme Court and the Demise of Popular Government* (1997); and Alexander M. Bickel, *The Supreme Court and the Idea of Progress* (1970).

81. See Samuel Moyn, *Counting on the Supreme Court to Uphold Key Rights Was Always a Mistake*, Wash. Post (June 17, 2022), https://perma.cc/K9FZ-ZN3F.

82. See generally Larry Kramer, *The People Themselves: Popular Constitutionalism and Judicial Review* (2005); and Mark Tushnet, *Taking the Constitution Away from the Courts* (2000). For an overview and critique, see Scott Douglas Gerber, *Popular Constitutionalism: The Contemporary Assault on Judicial Review*, in *A Distinct Judicial Power: The Origins of an Independent Judiciary, 1606–1787*, at 345–362 (2011). See also generally Jeremy Waldron, *The Core of the Case Against Judicial Review*, 115 Yale L.J. 1346 (2006).

83. See generally, for example, Lochner, 198 U.S. 45; Adkins, 261 U.S. 525.

84. See generally, for example, District of Columbia v. Heller, 554 U.S. 570 (2008).

85. See generally, for example, Gratz v. Bollinger, 539 U.S. 244 (2003).

86. See generally, for example, Citizens United v. Fed. Election Comm'n, 558 U.S. 310 (2010).

87. See generally, for example, Va. State Pharmacy Bd. v. Va. Citizens Consumer Council, 425 U.S. 748 (1976).

88. See generally, for example, California v. Texas, 141 S. Ct. 2104 (2021).

89. See generally, for example, West Virginia v. Envtl. Prot. Agency, 142 S. Ct. 2587 (2022).

90. See generally Jeremy Waldron, *The Core of the Case Against Judicial Review*, 115 Yale L.J. 1346 (2006). Waldron wrote:

> We are to imagine a society with (1) democratic institutions in reasonably good working order, including a representative legislature elected on the basis of universal adult suffrage; (2) a set of judicial institutions, again in reasonably good order, set up on a nonrepresentative basis to hear individual lawsuits, settle disputes, and uphold the rule of law; (3) a commitment on the part of most members of the society and most of its officials to the idea of individual and minority rights; and (4) persisting, substantial, and good faith disagreement about rights (i.e., about what the commitment to rights actually amounts to and what its implications are) among the members of the society who are committed to the idea of rights. (Supra at 1360)

91. I am phrasing all this with a deliberately high degree of abstraction. Different people would have different views about what counts as Athens and what counts as Babel. Religious conservatives might consider Athens to be something that Marxists abhor, and vice versa. In fact, different views about different approaches to constitutional law depend (I think) on projections about what judges are likely to do, which helps explain why political conservatives were drawn to Thayerism in the 1960s (but not so much today), and why those on the left tend to like Thayerism a lot more in 2024 than they did in the 1960s.

92. See Ely, supra note 74.

93. The categories are crude and intentionally so. We could imagine less crude alternatives, such as (1) originalism, (2) Thayerism, and (3) moral readings. Or (1) moral readings, (2) Thayerism, and (3) originalism. Or (1) democracy-reinforcement, (2) Thayerism, and (3) common good constitutionalism. The analysis in the text could be the same with options and preference orderings of these kinds.

CHAPTER 12

1. Shanto Iyengar, Guarav Sood, and Yphtach Lelkes, *Affect, Not Ideology: A Social Identity Perspective on Polarization*, 76 Pub. Opin. Q. 405 (2012).

2. Daryl J. Levinson and Richard H. Pildes, *Separation of Parties, Not Powers*, 119 Harv. L. Rev. 2311 (2006).

3. See Iyengar et al., supra note 1.

4. Id.

5. See, for example, Anthony Greenwald, Debbie E. McGhee, and Jordan L. K. Schwartz, *Measuring Individual Differences in Implicit Cognition: The Implicit Association Test*, 74 J. of Personality & Soc. Psych. 1464 (1998); and N. Sriram and Anthony G. Greenwald, *The Brief Implicit Association Test*, 56 Experimental Psych. 283 (2009)

("In eleven years since its introduction, the Implicit Association Test . . . has been used in several hundred studies to provide measures of association strengths.").

6. For example, Greenwald, McGhee, and Schwartz, supra note 5, at 1474; Scott A. Ottaway, Davis C. Hayden, and Mark A. Oakes, *Implicit Attitudes and Racism: Effects of Word Familiarity and Frequency on the Implicit Association Test*, 19 Soc. Cognition 97, 130 (2001); and Shanto Iyengar and Sean J. Westwood, *Fear and Loathing Across Party Lines: New Evidence on Group Polarization*, Working Paper 12 (2014).

7. See sources cited supra note 6.

8. This is a slight simplification of how the test works. See sources cited supra note 6.

9. Shanto Iyengar and Sean Westwood, *Fear and Loathing across Party Lines: New Evidence on Group Polarization*, 59 Am. J. Polit. Sci. 690 (2015).

10. Id. at 606.

11. See Iyengar et al., supra note 1, at 416 (showing a steady decrease in racial polarization from 1964 to 2008).

12. Iyengar et al., supra note 1, at 415–418.

13. Id.

14. Id.

15. Paul Taylor et al., Pew Social & Demographic Trends, The Rise of Intermarriage 7 (2012), http://www.pewsocialtrends.org/files/2012/02/SDT-Intermarriage-II.pdf.

16. Id. at 36.

17. See Frank Newport, *In U.S., 87% Approve of Black-White Marriage, vs. 4% in 1958*, Gallup (July 25, 2013), http://www.gallup.com/poll/163697/approve-marriage-blacks -whites.aspx.

18. Iyengar and Westwood, supra note 9.

19. Id.

20. Id.

21. Id.

22. Id.

23. Id.

24. Id.

25. Geoffrey D. Munro, Terell P. Lasane, and Scott P. Leary, *Political Partisan Prejudice: Selective Distortion and Weighting of Evaluative Categories in College Admissions Applications*, 40 J. Applied Soc. Psych. 2434, 2440 (2010).

26. Id. at 2444–2445.

27. Iyengar and Westwood, supra note 9.

28. Daniel Kahneman, Jack L. Knetsch, and Richard H. Thaler, *Fairness and the Assumptions of Economics*, 59 J. of Bus. S285 (1986).

29. Iyengar and Westwood, supra note 9.

30. Yphtach Lelkes and Sean J. Westwood, *The Nature and Limits of Partisan Prejudice*, Working Paper 2014.

31. Id. at 9.

32. Id. at 10.

33. Id. at 11.

34. Id. at 14.

35. Note, however, that there are significant qualifications to this finding, with some reluctance to discriminate along party lines. Id.

36. See Lilliana Mason, *"I Disrespectfully Agree": The Differential Effects of Partisan Sorting on Social and Issue Polarization*, 59 Am. J. of Poli. Sci. 138 (2015); Adrian Furnham, *Factors Relating to the Allocation of Medical Resources*, 11 J. Soc. Behav. & Personality 615, 620 (1996).

37. See Iyengar et al., supra note 1, at 422–423.

38. See Iyengar et al., supra note 1, at 425–427 (finding that residence in a battleground state during an election year correlates significantly with intensity of partisan affect, and that partisan affect increases significantly over the course of a campaign, especially in battleground states); and Guarav Sood, Shanto Iyengar, and Kyle Dropp, *Coming to Dislike Your Opponents: The Polarizing Impact of Political Campaigns*, Working Paper, April 2013 (finding that over the course of a campaign, partisans form more negative views of the opposing party, and the most strongly correlated feature is exposure to televised political advertising, especially negative ads).

39. For relevant discussion, see Cass R. Sunstein, Republic.com 2.0 (2007).

40. See Yphtach Lelkes, Shanto Iyengar, and Gaurav Sood, *The Hostile Audience: Selective Exposure to Partisan Sources and Affective Polarization*, Working Paper 2013 (finding that for partisans who pay attention to politics, cable access is correlated with greater partisan affect in years when cable carried partisan content, and further finding that the preference of partisans for choosing, between MSNBC and Fox News, the news sources amenable to their party "in and of itself—is sufficient to predict partisan animus, greater affect for in-party elites vis-à-vis out-party elites, greater social distance between partisans, and a preference for attack-oriented campaign rhetoric.").

41. See Levinson and Pildes, supra note 2.

42. Brendan Nyhan and Jason Reifler, *When Corrections Fail: The Persistence of Political Misperceptions*, 32 Pol. Behav. 303, 312 (2010).

43. Id. at 312–313.

44. Id. at 314.

45. Id. at 314–315.

46. Id. at 320.

47. Brendan Nyhan, Jason Reifler, and Peter A. Ubel, *The Hazards of Correcting Myths About Health Care Reform*, 51 Med. Care 127, 127 (2013).

48. Id. at 129–130.

49. Id.

50. Id.

51. Nyhan and Reifler, supra note 42, at 321.

52. Id. at 321–322.

53. Thomas Wood and Ethan Porter, *The Elusive Backfire Effect: Mass Attitudes' Steadfast Factual Adherence*, 41 Political Behav. 135 (2019).

54. See Geoffrey Cohen, *Party Over Policy*, 85 J. Pers. Soc. Psychol. 808 (2003).

55. Id.

INDEX

Abdication, 60–63

Abortion, 100–102, 106, 108

Absolutism, 25, 82

Absurdity Canon, 92, 148n62

Accountability
deliberative democracy and, 3
executive power and, 21, 23–24
Grand Narrative and, 68
legislative power and, 13

Adjudication
executive power and, 20, 24
Grand Narrative and, 61–74, 141n76
legislative power and, 10–11

Administrative Procedure Act (APA), 66

Affirmative action, 100–101, 105–108

Affordable Care Act, 24, 101, 107, 122–123

AFL-CIO, 47, 138n23, 144n19, 148n62

African Americans, 2, 114–116

Air pollution, 21, 42, 127

Alabama Association of Realtors v. Department of Health & Human Services, 148n71

Alito, Samuel, 68, 72

American Revolution, 3

American Trucking case, 62, 74

Ameron, Inc. v. Army Corps of Engineers, 137–138n10

Article I
courts and, 24
executive power and, 20, 22
freedom and, 3–4
Grand Narrative and, 59–62, 68–71, 74
legislative power and, 3–4, 20, 22, 24, 59–62, 68–71, 74, 85, 87, 91
major questions doctrine and, 85, 87, 91
section 1 of, 3, 22–24, 68, 71, 87, 91
Vesting Clause of, 69, 85

Article II
executive power and, 3, 30, 32–33
freedom and, 3
Grand Narrative and, 59–64, 70, 74
immunity and, 30, 32–33
removal cases and, 30
section 1 of, 3

Article III
courts and, 3, 5, 20, 60, 66–71
executive power and, 20
freedom and, 3, 5
Grand Narrative and, 59–71, 74
judicial power and, 3, 5, 20, 60, 69
legislative power and, 3–5, 66
section 1 of, 3

Attorney general, 18, 30, 32–33, 45, 67

Authoritarianism, 3, 121
Avoidance Canon, 14, 91–92, 148n60, 148n62

Bandwidth neglect, 39
Barrett, Amy Coney
  Gorsuch and, 87–88, 91–94, 148n71
  major questions doctrine and, 86–94, 148n71
  strong-form canons and, 87–88
  Wittgenstein and, 86, 90–93, 148n71
Bias
  deliberative democracy and, 49, 55
  executive power and, 18–19, 44
  group polarization and, 40, 57
  happy talk and, 40, 57
  Office of Legal Counsel and, 19
  partyism and, 115
  reelection and, 46
Bicameralism, 21, 68
Bickel, Alexander, 101, 103–104, 133n17, 151n73
Biden, Hunter, 30
Biden, Joe, 37, 40, 51, 94, 113, 125
Biden v. Nebraska, 93
Bill of Rights, 2, 152n79
Birth control, 103
Black, Hugo, 102
Bolling v. Sharpe, 98, 102–103
Bowen v. Georgetown University Hospital, 134n22, 143n1
Bowie, Nikolas, 133n12
Brandeis, Louis, 99, 101, 109
Breyer, Stephen, 106
Brown v. Board of Education, 102–103
Burkeanism, 49, 72–74, 140n72
Bush, George W., 35, 122–123
Bush v. Gore, 35

Calabresi, Steven G., 152n79
Carbon emissions, 51, 55
Cardozo, Benjamin N., 109
Carter, Jimmy, 19

Checks and balances, 5–6, 121, 152n79
Chevron v. NRDC, 66, 74
Citizens United v. FEC, 98
Civil rights, 9, 45, 120
Clean Air Act (CAA), 17–18, 24, 89, 93
Climate change
  deliberative democracy and, 51, 55
  executive power and, 21
  Grand Narrative and, 71
  partyism and, 119
Clinton v. Jones, 135n2
Coercion, 2, 10, 141n76
Cohen, Felix, 103
Commerce Clause, 101
Common law, 23–24, 83, 146n39
Communists, 114, 117–118
Conservativism
  deliberative democracy and, 55
  Fox News and, 120, 123, 155n40
  partyism and, 119–123
  religious, 153n91
  Thayerism and, 106–107
Consumer Financial Protection Bureau, 64
Consumer Product Safety Commission, 60
Core of the Case Against Judicial Review, The (Waldron), 153n90
Council of Economic Advisers, 50–52, 54
Council on Environmental Quality, 51
Courts
  Article I and, 24
  Article III and, 3, 5, 20, 60–61, 65–71
  immunity and, 27–36
  independence of, 10, 17, 19, 60–66, 106, 110, 121, 142n92
  inferior, 3, 60
  judicial power, 3 (see also Judicial power)
  liberty and, 24–25
  Nazis and, 19
  prosecutorial discretion and, 7

rule of law and, 25
Trump and, 27–36, 135n3, 136n24
tyranny and, 24–25
U.S. Constitution and, 24–25
U.S. Supreme Court, 35 (*see also* U.S. Supreme Court)
Criminal law, 127
Due Process Clause, 79–80, 100, 102, 106, 108, 143n11
executive power and, 17, 19, 21
Ex Post Facto Clause, 79–80
immunity and, 27, 30–34, 36
legislative power and, 7–10, 8, 14
Magna Carta of, 1–2
nondelegation doctrine and, 79–80
pardons and, 28–32, 136n17
retroactive application and, 79, 83
Thayerism and, 103
Crowell v. Benson, 20, 61–62, 66–67, 71, 74

Death panels, 122–123
Death penalty, 101
Decision of 1789, 63–64
Deep state, 38–40, 49
Deliberative democracy
accountability and, 3
bias and, 49, 55
Burkeanism and, 49, 72–74, 140n72
climate change and, 51, 55
conservatism and, 55
constraint and, 56–57
deep state and, 49
Democrats and, 56–57
discretion and, 56
draft rules and, 50, 52
elections and, 49
environmental issues and, 51
executive power and, 21–25, 49–57
experts and, 49–51, 54–56
Grand Narrative and, 70
House of Representatives and, 49
idealized view of, 54–56

information and, 51–57
interest groups and, 49, 55–56
judicial power and, 53–57
labor and, 52
learning, 53–54
legal issues and, 51–52, 54, 56
liberty and, 57
partyism and, 113
protection of, 6
reality and, 50–51
regulation and, 51–53, 56
Republicans and, 55–57
rule of law and, 57
self-government and, 22
Senate and, 50
tradition and, 49
Trump and, 51, 54–55
U.S. Constitution and, 3, 56
White House and, 50, 54–55
Democracy and Distrust (Ely), 35
Democratic disorder, 35
Democrats
Big Business and, 114
deliberative democracy and, 56–57
executive power and, 43, 47
partyism and, 113–124
Department of Agriculture, 8, 51–52
Department of Commerce, 51–52
Department of Energy, 50–52
Department of Health and Human Services, 8
Department of Homeland Security, 8, 10, 18, 140n71
Department of Justice
attorney general and, 18, 30, 32–33, 45, 67
deliberative democracy and, 54
executive power and, 19, 31–33
immunity and, 33
legislative power and, 8
Office of Legal Counsel, 18–19
Department of Labor, 8, 52
Department of State, 8, 50, 52

Department of the Treasury, 50–52
Department of Transportation, 51
Discretion
    deliberative democracy and, 56
    executive power and, 22, 128
    Grand Narrative and, 60–62, 67,
        70–74
    judicial power and, 24–25, 29
    legislative power and, 7–9
    major questions doctrine and, 88,
        91, 93
    nondelegation doctrine and, 78, 82
    Thayerism and, 101
Discrimination
    affirmative action and, 100–101,
        105–108
    liberty and, 9
    partyism and, 155n35
    racial, 99, 103, 105–106
    sex, 99, 106, 108
    strict scrutiny and, 105
Domestic Policy Council, 52
Douglas, William O., 102–103
Draft rules, 50, 52
Dred Scott v. Sandford, 137n35
Duelfer Report, 122
Due Process Clause
    nondelegation doctrine and, 79–80,
        143n11
    retroactive application and, 79
    Thayerism and, 100, 102, 106, 108

Education, 9, 17, 102
EEOC v. Arabian American Oil Co.,
        134n23
Elections
    deliberative democracy and, 49
    executive power and, 33, 35–36,
        45–48
    fraud in, 33
    immunity and, 33, 35–36
    legislative power and, 14, 45–48
    partyism and, 155n38

reelection, 10, 14, 45–48
    Thayerism and, 103
Ely, John Hart, 35, 103–105
Employment, 9, 42, 108, 127, 143n11
Environmental issues
    air pollution, 21, 42, 127
    carbon emissions, 51, 55
    Clean Air Act (CAA), 17–18, 24, 89,
        93
    cost of, 41–42
    deliberative democracy, 51
    executive power, 21–22, 34, 39, 41–
        42, 45, 47
    experts, 45
    major questions doctrine, 89
    mercury, 38, 40–41, 56
    ozone, 18, 40–42, 51, 56
Environmental Protection Agency
    (EPA), 8, 10, 17–18, 46, 51, 89
Epistemic argument, 23–24, 39, 48,
        55–56
Equality
    affirmative action and, 100–101,
        105–108
    nondelegation doctrine and, 78
    Thayerism and, 102
    U.S. Constitution and, 2
Equal Protection Clause, 8, 100, 106
Equities, 51, 62
Erie R.R. Co. v. Tompkins, 23
European Convention on Human
        Rights, 77–78
Executive Office of the President, 50, 52
Executive power
    accountability and, 21, 23–24
    adjudication and, 20, 24
    Article I and, 20, 22
    Article II and, 3, 30, 32–33
    Article III and, 20
    bias and, 18–19, 44
    climate change and, 21
    criminal law and, 17, 19, 21
    danger of, 37–48

deep state and, 38–40, 49

deliberative democracy and, 21–25, 49–57

Democrats and, 43, 47

discretion and, 22, 128, 145n17

elections and, 33, 35–36, 45–48

environmental issues and, 21–22, 34, 39, 41–42, 45, 47

experts and, 45–48

freedom and, 17

Grand Narrative and, 59–71

group polarization and, 21, 40

Hamilton and, 11–15, 19

happy talk and, 40, 57

ideology and, 44

immigration and, 21, 23, 34, 38, 40–41, 46–47

immunity and, 27–37, 128, 135nn2–3

information and, 37–47

interest groups and, 39–40, 44, 48

interpretation of, 17–20

judicial power and, 17–25, 29, 35–36, 42–43, 128, 135n3, 136n24

labor and, 46–47

legal issues and, 18–19

legislative power and, 7–10, 20–22, 30, 32–33, 39, 41–42, 47–48, 128

liberty and, 17–22, 40, 132n27

limitations of, 4–6, 17–22

major questions doctrine and, 85, 89, 92–94

nondelegation doctrine and, 77–84

pardons and, 28–32, 136n17

partyism and, 121

polarization and, 21, 40, 42, 46

public health and, 41, 45–46

public meaning originalists and, 5, 32

reform and, 21, 41

regulation and, 17–18, 30, 40–42, 46–48

reprieves and, 28, 31

Republicans and, 43, 47

rule of law and, 18–19

self-government and, 22, 25

Take Care Clause, 18

Thayerism and, 96, 99

tradition and, 7, 19–20

tyranny and, 128

unitary executive and, 63–65

unquestionable power and, 27–28

unreviewability and, 29

U.S. Constitution and, 18–19

Experts

deliberative democracy and, 49–51, 54–56

environmental issues, 45

executive power and, 45–48

foreign policy, 45

Grand Narrative and, 64–65

health care, 45

information and, 45–51, 54–56, 64–65, 83, 108, 147n41, 152n79

major questions doctrine and, 147n41

nondelegation doctrine and, 83

Thayerism and, 108, 152n79

Ex Post Facto Clause, 79–80

Extraterritoriality

legislative power and, 14, 134n23

major questions doctrine and, 91

nondelegation doctrine and, 78, 80, 83, 143n13

Fascism, 6, 9

FDA v. Brown & Williamson Tobacco Corp., 93, 144n1, 148n64

Federal Communications Commission (FCC), 60, 64–65, 88, 138n10, 145n16

Federalist Society, 47

Federal Reserve Board, 60, 64

Federal Trade Commission (FTC), 59–60, 65, 138n10, 139n42

Fifth Amendment, 100, 143n11

First Amendment, 13, 100, 102, 106

Foreign policy, 45
Fourteenth Amendment, 102, 104
Fourth branch of government, 59–60, 69, 137–138n10
Fox News, 120, 123, 155n40
Frankfurter, Felix, 98–99, 101–103, 109, 151n59
Fraud, 33
Freedom
    Article I and, 3–4
    Article II and, 3
    executive power and, 17
    immunity and, 2
    judicial power and, 3–6
    legislative power and, 3, 8
    liberty and, 6
    from official incursion, 2
    prosecutorial discretion and, 7
    rule of law and, 2
    sovereignty and, 2
    textualism and, 4
    Thayerism and, 109
    tradition and, 5
    tyranny and, 2–3
    U.S. Constitution and, 2–6
Freedom from fear, 2
Freedom from violence, 128
Freedom of religion, 2, 109
Freedom of speech, 2, 13, 79, 102, 108–109
Free Enterprise Fund case, 63–64
Free foot, 73, 96–97
FTC v. Ruberoid Co., 59, 138n10

Game theory, 110, 116
Gore, Al, 35
Gorsuch, Neil
    Barrett and, 87–88, 91–94, 148–149n71
    common law and, 146n39
    Grand Narrative and, 67–69, 71
    major questions doctrine and, 85–88, 94

U.S. Supreme Court and, 67–69, 71, 85–88, 94, 145n8, 146n39, 148–149n71
Grand Narrative
    abdication and, 60–63
    accountability and, 68
    adjudication and, 61–74, 141n76
    Article I and, 59–62, 68–71, 74
    Article II and, 59–64, 70, 74
    Article III and, 59–71, 74
    Burkeanism and, 72–74, 140n72
    climate change and, 71
    counternarratives and, 69–74
    Decision of 1789 and, 63–64
    deliberative democracy and, 70
    discretion and, 60–62, 67, 70–74
    executive power and, 59–71
    experts and, 64–65
    foundations of, 74–75
    fourth branch of government and, 59–60, 69, 137–138n10
    Gorsuch and, 67–69, 71
    immunity and, 69
    independence and, 60, 63–64, 138n10
    information and, 139n40
    interpretation and, 65–66, 72–74
    judicial power and, 59–75, 139n39, 139n42, 141n76, 142n92
    labor and, 60, 65
    legal issues and, 59, 66, 75, 137–138n10, 142n96
    legislative power and, 60, 63–69, 73–74
    liberty and, 70
    major questions doctrine and, 68–69, 74
    New Deal and, 59–61, 69
    power of, 69
    in practice, 63–69
    pragmatism and, 73–74, 140n72
    public health and, 62
    public meaning originalists and, 70–72, 74

public rights exception and, 66–67, 71, 74
questioning, 74–75
reform and, 72
regulation and, 60, 62, 65, 71
rejection of, 72–73
Schechter Poultry v. United States, 60, 67
Seila Law, 64–66, 74, 138n16
sovereignty and, 69
Take Care Clause, 63–64
Thayerism and, 73–74
tradition and, 61, 70, 72, 138n10
Trump and, 65
unitary executive and, 63–65
U.S. Constitution and, 59–74
Great Society, 60
Gridlock, 21, 117, 124–125
Group polarization, 21, 40
Gundy v. United States, 67

Hamilton, Alexander, 11–15, 19
Hand, Learned, 98, 109, 150n33
Happy talk, 40, 57
Harlan, John Marshall, 103
Hayek, Friedrich, 53
Heritage Foundation, 48
Hitler, Adolph, 1–3, 6, 127
"Hitler Is Supreme Under Enabling Act" (*New York Times*), 1
Holmes, Oliver Wendell, 95, 99, 101–102, 109
Hostile Audience: The: Selective Exposure to Partisan Sources and Affective Polarization (Lelkes, Iyengar, and Sood), 155n40
House of Representatives
Article I and, 3
bicameralism and, 21, 68
deliberative democracy and, 49
impeachment and, 6, 133n9
OIRA and, 47–48
partyism and, 124
reelection and, 47

Human Rights Act, 77–78
Humphrey's Executor v. United States, 61–65, 74, 139n39, 139n42
Hussein, Saddam, 122

Ideology
conservativism, 55, 106, 119–123, 153n91
executive power and, 44
Iraq War and, 122
liberalism, 1–3, 106–107, 119–123
major questions doctrine and, 89
partyism and, 119–124
Immigration
executive power and, 21, 23, 34, 38, 40–41, 46–47
partyism and, 120
seriousness of, 127
Immunity
absolute, 30, 135n3
Article II and, 30, 32–33
criminal law and, 27, 30–34, 36
democratic disorder and, 35
Department of Justice and, 33
elections and, 33, 35–36
executive power and, 27–37
freedom and, 2
Grand Narrative and, 69
judicial power and, 27–36, 128, 135n3
legal issues and, 2, 9, 36
legislative power and, 9, 30, 32–33
major questions doctrine and, 85
nondelegation doctrine and, 81
pardons and, 28–32, 136n17
possible impact of, 32–34
pragmatism and, 35–36
presidential, 27–36, 128, 135nn2–3
presumptive, 135n3
public meaning originalists and, 32
regulation and, 30
sovereignty and, 69
Trump v. United States, 27–36

Immunity (cont.)
  unquestionable power and, 27–28
  unreviewability and, 29
  U.S. Constitution and, 27–36
  U.S. Supreme Court and, 27–36
  Youngstown and, 28
Impeachment, 6, 31, 99, 133n9
Implicit association test (IAT), 114–115,
    154n5
Independence
  agency, 63
  courts and, 10, 17, 19, 60–66, 106,
    110, 121, 142n92
  degrees of, 10
  Grand Narrative and, 60, 63–64,
    137–138n10
  judicial, 11, 14, 17, 19, 60–66, 106,
    110, 121, 142n92
  Thayerism and, 96
  U.S. Constitution and, 11–14, 60–66,
    96, 99, 101, 106, 110, 128, 142n92
Inflation, 21, 24, 127
Information
  acquisition of, 42–43
  bandwidth neglect and, 39
  classified, 7
  constraint and, 56–57
  deficit in, 38–39
  deliberative democracy and, 51–57
  elections and, 45–48
  executive power and, 37–47
  experts and, 45–51, 54–56, 64–65, 83,
    108, 147n41, 152n79
  Grand Narrative and, 139n40
  Hayek and, 53
  judicial power and, 23, 38, 43–44, 46
  legal issues and, 43–44
  legislative power and, 45–48
  major questions doctrine and, 90
  OIRA and, 8, 47–48, 51–53
  partyism and, 117, 121–124
  public health and, 40–43
  regulation and, 40–43

  technical, 37–38, 43, 46, 51, 90
  Thayerism and, 104
INS v. Chadha, 63
Interest groups
  deliberative democracy and, 49,
    55–56
  executive power and, 39–40, 44, 48
  legislative power and, 39
  liberty and, 40
Internal Revenue Service (IRS), 10
Interpretation
  executive power and, 17–20
  Grand Narrative and, 65–66, 72–74
  independent, 142n92
  judicial power and, 11–14, 17–18, 20,
    25, 66, 92, 97–98, 128, 142n92
  legislative power and, 11–14
  major questions doctrine and, 87–88,
    92–94
  nondelegation doctrine and, 77, 79–
    81, 143n2
  Thayerism and, 95–101, 104, 145n8,
    146n22
  U.S. Constitution and, 4–5, 11–14,
    25, 66, 72–74, 79–80, 87, 93–101,
    104, 106, 128, 132n21, 141n85,
    142n92, 146n39
Interpreting Statutes in the Regulatory State
    (Sunstein), 146n22
Interracial marriage, 115
Iraq War, 122
Iyengar, Shanto, 115–116, 120, 154n9,
    155n38, 155n40

Jackson, Robert, 7–8, 28–29, 34, 59
Jim Crow segregation, 152n79
Judicial power
  adjudication, 10–11, 20, 24, 61–74,
    141n76
  Article III and, 3, 5, 20, 60, 69
  attorney general and, 18, 30, 32–33,
    45, 67
  deep state and, 39

deference of, 53–54, 145n4
deliberative democracy and, 53–57
discretion and, 24–25, 29
epistemic argument and, 23
executive power and, 17–25, 29, 35–
    36, 42–43, 128, 135n3, 136n24
freedom and, 3–6
Grand Narrative and, 59–75, 139n39,
    139n42, 141n76, 142n92
immunity and, 27–36, 128, 135n3
information and, 23, 38, 43–44, 46
interpretation and, 11–14, 17–18, 20,
    25, 66, 92, 97–98, 128, 142n92
legislative power and, 10–15, 23–25,
    128
limitations of, 4–6, 23–25
major questions doctrine and, 87–94,
    147n41
Nazis and, 1–3
nondelegation doctrine and, 77–83,
    144n14
partyism and, 121, 125
quasi-authority and, 65
reasonable doubt and, 73, 97–101,
    104–106
regulation and, 24–25
retroactive application and, 79, 83
review, 13–15, 56–57, 69, 96, 98, 101,
    107, 140n71, 152n79, 153n90
Senate and, 6
Thayerism and, 73, 95–111
tradition and, 23
Trump and, 27–33, 65, 94, 135n3,
    136n24

Kagan, Elena, 147n41
Kent v. Dulles, 148n60

Labor
    AFL-CIO and, 47, 144n19, 148n62
    deep state and, 38
    deliberative democracy and, 52
    Department of Labor, 8, 52

employment and, 9, 42, 108, 127,
    143n11
executive power and, 46–47
Grand Narrative and, 60, 65
National Labor Relations Board
    (NLRB), 20, 60, 65
partyism and, 115–117
prejudice and, 115–117
Thayerism and, 102
unions and, 46–47, 138n23, 144n19,
    148n62
Lankford, James, 48
Legal issues. See also specific article
    AFL-CIO v. American Petroleum
        Institute, 138n23, 144n19, 148n62
    Alabama Association of Realtors v.
        Department of Health & Human
        Services, 148n71
    amendments, 13, 67, 100, 102, 104,
        106, 138n22, 143n11
    American Trucking, 62, 74
    Ameron, Inc. v. Army Corps of
        Engineers, 137–138n10
    attorney general and, 18, 30, 32–33,
        45, 67
    Biden v. Nebraska, 93
    Bolling v. Sharpe, 98, 102–103
    Bowen v. Georgetown University
        Hospital, 134n22, 143n1
    Brown v. Board of Education, 102–103
    Bush v. Gore, 35
    Chevron v. NRDC, 66, 74
    Citizens United v. FEC, 98
    Clinton v. Jones, 135n2
    common law, 23–24, 83, 146n39
    courts, 25, 27 (see also Courts)
    Crowell v. Benson, 20, 61–62, 66–67,
        71, 74
    deliberative democracy, 51–52, 54, 56
    Due Process Clause, 79–80, 100, 102,
        106, 108, 143n11
    EEOC v. Arabian American Oil Co.,
        134n23

Legal issues (cont.)
Erie case, 23
executive power, 18–19
Ex Post Facto Clause, 79–80
FDA v. Brown & Williamson Tobacco
Corp., 93, 144n1, 148n64
Free Enterprise Fund, 63–64
FTC v. Ruberoid Co., 59, 138n10
Grand Narrative, 59, 66, 75, 137–
138n10, 142n96
Gundy v. United States, 68
Humphrey's Executor v. United States,
61–65, 74, 139n39, 139n42
immunity, 2, 9, 36
information, 43–44
INS v. Chadha, 63
interpretation, 4 (see also
Interpretation)
Kent v. Dulles, 148n60
legislative power, 12, 133n12
Lochner v. New York, 97, 102
Loper Bright Enterprises v. Raimondo,
66, 138n16, 139n46, 139n48
McCulloch v. Maryland, 142n96
Marbury v. Madison, 66, 96, 133n10
MCI, 88, 93, 146n32
Michigan Citizens for an Independent
Press v. Thornburg, 144n17
Muscogee (Creek) Nation v. Hodel,
143n2
Myers v. United States, 64
Nazi justification, 1
nondelegation doctrine, 77, 91–92,
143n13
Office of Legal Counsel, 18–19
retroactive application, 79, 83,
134n22
Roe v. Wade, 105
Schechter Poultry v. United States, 60,
67
Schmidt on, 1–2, 6, 17, 20–21
SEC v. Jarkesy, 59, 67, 71
Seila Law, 64–66, 74, 138n16

strict scrutiny, 105
Take Care Clause, 18, 63–64
Thayerism, 98, 101–102, 108
Trump v. Anderson, 35–36
Trump v. United States, 27–36
United States v. Carolene Products, 104
United States v. Klein, 29–30
unreviewability, 29
U.S. Constitution, 3 (see also U.S.
Constitution)
Usery v. Turner Elkhorn Mining, 143n11
West Virginia v. EPA, 68
Youngstown Sheet & Steel Tube Co. v.
Sawyer, 21, 28, 30
Legislative power
accountability and, 13
adjudication and, 10–11
Article I and, 3–4, 20, 22, 24, 59–62,
68–71, 74, 85, 87, 91
Article III and, 3–5, 66
bicameralism and, 21, 68
criminal law and, 7–10, 8, 14
deep state and, 39
discretion and, 7–9
elections and, 14, 45–48
executive power and, 7–10, 20–22,
30, 32–33, 39, 41–42, 47–48, 128
extraterritoriality and, 14, 134n23
freedom and, 3, 8
Grand Narrative and, 60, 63–69,
73–74
Hamilton and, 11–15, 19
immunity and, 9, 30, 32–33
impeachment, 6, 31, 99, 133n9
information and, 45–48
interest groups and, 39
interpretation of, 11–14
judicial power and, 10–15, 23–25, 128
legal issues and, 12, 133n12
liberty and, 7–11, 15, 132n27
limitations of, 4–15
major questions doctrine and, 85, 94
Nazis and, 1–3, 127

New Deal and, 9
nondelegation doctrine and, 77–84
partyism and, 113, 119, 121, 124–125
public health and, 8–9
public meaning originalists and,
    12–13
reasonable doubt and, 73, 97–99, 101
regulation and, 8–10
rule of law and, 13–15
taxes and, 7
Thayerism and, 95–104, 107–110
tradition and, 7, 10–11, 14
unreviewability and, 29
U.S. Constitution and, 11–15
use of term, 20–21
Lelkes, Yphtach, 155n40
Levinson, Daryl, 113, 121
Liberalism
    MSNBC and, 120, 155n40
    Nazis and, 1–3
    partyism and, 119–123
    Schmidt on, 1–2
    Thayerism and, 106–107
    tradition of, 3
    U.S. Constitution and, 2
Liberty
    courts and, 24–25
    deliberative democracy and, 57
    executive power and, 17–22, 40,
        132n27
    freedom and, 6
    Grand Narrative and, 70
    interest groups and, 40
    legislative power and, 7–11, 15,
        132n27
    Lincoln on, 2–3
    nondelegation doctrine and, 78–79
    partyism and, 113, 121, 128
    religious, 79
    right conception of, 9–10
    self-government and, 2–3, 22, 25,
        105
    sovereignty and, 2

Thayerism and, 98
U.S. Constitution and, 2, 15, 25, 78–
    79, 98
Liberty Lies in the Hearts of Men and
    Women (Hand), 150n33
Lincoln, Abraham, 2–3, 29
Lochner v. New York, 97, 102
Locke, John, 85, 145n6, 148n71
Loper Bright Enterprises v. Raimondo, 66,
    138n16, 139n46, 139n48

Madison, James
    checks and balances of, 152n79
    Marbury v. Madison and, 66, 96,
        133n10
    self-government and, 3
    tyranny and, 24
    U.S. Constitution and, 3, 66, 96,
        152n79
Major questions doctrine
    Absurdity Canon and, 92, 148n62
    Article I and, 85, 87, 91
    Avoidance Canon and, 91–92,
        148n60, 148n62
    Barrett and, 86–94, 148n71
    basic premise of, 91
    challenges to, 88–92
    clear-statement rules and, 87
    discretion and, 88, 91, 93
    environmental issues and, 89
    executive power and, 85, 89, 92–94
    experts and, 147n41
    extraterritoriality and, 91
    Gorsuch and, 85–88, 94, 145n8,
        146n39, 148n71
    Grand Narrative and, 68–69, 74
    ideology and, 89
    immunity and, 85
    information and, 90
    interpretation and, 87–88, 92–94
    judicial power and, 87–94, 147n41
    legislative power and, 85, 94
    Locke and, 85

Major questions doctrine (cont.)
  public health and, 89
  regulation and, 89
  religion and, 91
  sovereignty and, 85
  strong-form canons and, 87–88
  taxes and, 87
  textualism and, 87–88, 91–93,
    146n32
  tradition and, 92–93
  U.S. Constitution and, 85, 87–88,
    91–93
  vacillation over, 92–94
  Wittgenstein and, 86–93, 148n71
Marbury v. Madison, 66, 96, 133n10
Marriage, 101, 103, 115
Marshall, John, 66, 96
McCulloch v. Maryland, 142n96
*MCI Telecomms. Corp v. American
    Telephone and Telegraph Corp.*, 88,
    93, 146n32
Media, 39, 120, 122
Mercury, 38, 40–41, 56
*Michigan Citizens for an Independent Press
    v. Thornburg*, 144n17
Minority rights, 68, 104, 108, 124–125,
    153n90
Montesquieu, 132n27
MSNBC, 120, 155n40
Muscogee (Creek) Nation v. Hodel, 143n2
Myers v. United States, 64
Myths, 55, 70–71, 141n76, 156n47

National Association of Manufacturers,
    46–47
National Economic Council, 50–52
National Highway Traffic Safety
    Administration, 45
National Labor Relations Board (NLRB),
    20, 60, 65
National Security Council, 52
National Traffic and Motor Vehicle
    Safety Act, 90

Native Americans, 67, 78, 81, 143n2,
    144n14
Natural Resources Defense Council, 47
Nazis
  courts and, 19
  Hitler, 1–3, 6, 127
  judicial power and, 1–3
  legislative power and, 1–3, 127
  liberalism and, 1–3
  Night of the Long Knives and, 1
  partyism and, 114, 118
  racial prejudice and, 114
  Schmidt on, 1–3, 6, 15, 17, 20–21, 28
Neutrality, 101–103
New Deal
  Grand Narrative and, 59–61, 69
  legislative power and, 9
  Thayerism and, 102
New York Times, 1, 123
Night of the Long Knives, 1
Nondelegation doctrine
  bypassing, 143n7
  criminal law and, 79–80
  discretion and, 78, 82
  Due Process Clause and, 79–80,
    143n11
  equality and, 78
  executive power and, 77–84
  experts and, 83
  extraterritoriality and, 78, 80, 83,
    143n13
  foreign relations and, 143n13
  immunity and, 81
  institutions and, 82–84
  interpretation and, 77, 79–81, 143n2
  judicial power and, 77–83, 144n14
  legal issues and, 77, 91–92, 143n13
  legislative power and, 77–84
  liberty and, 78–79
  regulation and, 82–83, 144n19
  religion and, 79
  rights and, 82–84
  sovereignty and, 80–81

taxes and, 81
U.S. Constitution and, 78–83
Nuclear Regulatory Commission, 60, 65

Obama, Barack, 8–9, 40, 125
Office of Information and Regulatory
    Affairs (OIRA), 8, 47–48, 51–53
Office of Legal Counsel, 18–19
Office of Management and Budget, 50–
    52, 54
Office of Science and Technology Policy,
    51
Office of the Chief of Staff, 52
Office of the United States Trade
    Representative, 52
Office of the Vice President, 52
One-party rule, 121, 124
Originalism and James Bradley Thayer
    (Calabresi), 152n79
*Origin and Scope of the American Doctrine
    of Constitutional Law, The* (Thayer),
    149n1
Ozone, 18, 40–42, 51, 56

Palin, Sarah, 122–123
Pandemics, 22, 38, 147n41
Pardons, 28–32, 136n17
Partyism
    bias and, 115
    campaigns and, 120
    causes of, 119–120
    checks and balances, 121
    climate change and, 119
    conservatism and, 119–123
    corrections and, 122–123
    deliberative democracy and, 113
    Democrats and, 113–124
    discrimination and, 155n35
    effects of, 117–125
    elections and, 155n38
    executive power and, 121
    gridlock and, 21, 117, 124–125
    harm of, 113

House of Representatives and, 124
    ideology and, 119–124
    immigration and, 120
    implicit association test (IAT) and,
        114–115, 154n5
    information and, 117, 121–124
    judicial power and, 121, 125
    labor and, 115–117
    legislative power and, 113, 119, 121,
        124–125
    liberalism and, 119–123
    liberty and, 113, 121, 128
    marriage and, 115
    media and, 39, 120, 122
    Nazis and, 114, 118
    one-party rule, 121, 124
    polarization and, 120–123
    prejudice and, 113–119
    racial issues and, 114–116
    reform and, 123–124
    Republicans and, 113–124
    Senate and, 124
    sexism and, 113, 117–118
    taxes and, 122
    thermometer ratings and, 114
    Trump and, 113, 125
    trust game and, 116
    tyranny and, 128
    White House and, 124
Pildes, Richard, 113, 121
Polarization
    executive power and, 21, 40, 42, 46
    group, 21, 40
    media and, 155n40
    partyism and, 120–123
Popular constitutionalism, 107
Posner, Richard, 82
Pragmatism, 35, 73–74, 140n72
Prejudice
    corrections and, 122–123
    equality and, 2, 78, 102
    implicit association test (IAT) and,
        114–115, 154n5

Prejudice (cont.)
  increase of, 115
  labor and, 115–117
  marriage and, 115
  minorities and, 68, 104, 108, 124–
    125, 153n90
  one-party rule, 121, 124
  partyism and, 113–119
  racial, 104, 114–115
  segregation, 102, 106, 108, 120,
    152n70
  trust game and, 116
Principals committee, 50
Prosecutorial discretion, 7
Public health, 22, 38, 147n41
  Affordable Care Act, 24, 101, 107,
    122–123
  Department of Health and Human
    Services, 8
  environmental issues, 41 (*see also*
    Environmental issues)
  executive power and, 41, 45–46
  Grand Narrative and, 62
  information and, 40–43
  legislative power and, 8–9
  major questions doctrine and, 89
  safety and, 89 (*see also* Safety)
  seriousness of, 127
  Thayerism and, 107
Public meaning originalists
  executive power and, 5, 32
  Grand Narrative and, 70–72, 74,
    141n74
  immunity and, 32
  legislative power and, 12–13
  Thayerism and, 100, 106, 152n70,
    152n79
Public rights exception, 66–67, 71, 74
Putin, Vladimir, 127

Racial issues
  affirmative action, 100–101, 105–108
  African Americans, 2, 114–116
  Bolling v. Sharpe, 98, 102–103
  Brown v. Board of Education, 102–103
  decreased polarization, 154n11
  discrimination, 99, 103, 105–106
  Douglas, 103
  equality, 2, 78, 102
  implicit association test (IAT), 114–
    115, 154n5
  interracial marriage, 115
  labor, 115–117
  minorities, 68, 104, 108, 124–125,
    153n90
  Native Americans, 67, 78, 81, 143n2,
    144n14
  Nazis, 114
  partyism, 114–116
  prejudice, 104, 114–115
  segregation, 102, 106, 108, 120,
    152n70
Reagan, Ronald, 19
Reasonable doubt
  judicial power and, 73, 97–99, 101,
    104–106
  legislative power and, 73, 97–99, 101
  Thayerism and, 73, 95–101, 104–106
  U.S. Constitution and, 73, 95–101,
    104–105
Reelection, 10, 14, 45–48
Reform
  executive power and, 21, 41
  Grand Narrative and, 72
  partyism and, 123–124
  Thayerism and, 98
Regulation
  deliberative democracy and, 51–53,
    56
  draft rules and, 50, 52
  executive power and, 17–18, 30, 40–
    42, 46–48
  FTC and, 59, 60, 65, 138n10, 139n42
  Grand Narrative and, 60, 62, 65, 71
  Great Society and, 60
  immunity and, 30

judicial power and, 24–25
legislative power and, 8–10
major questions doctrine and, 89
National Traffic and Motor Vehicle
Safety Act, 90
New Deal and, 60
nondelegation doctrine and, 82–83,
144n19
Nuclear Regulatory Commission, 60,
65
OIRA and, 51–53
retroactive application and, 79, 83
Schechter Poultry v. United States, 60,
67
Thayerism and, 99–102, 107
Religion
conservatism and, 153n91
freedom of, 2, 109
liberty and, 79
major questions doctrine and, 91
nondelegation doctrine and, 79
textualism and, 91
Thayerism and, 104, 108–109,
153n91
Renan, Daphna, 133n12
Reprieves, 28, 31
Republicans
deliberative democracy and, 55–57
executive power and, 43, 47
partyism and, 113–124
Thayerism and, 105
welfare and, 114
Retroactive application, 79, 83, 134n22
Roberts, John, 67, 138n10, 138n16
Roe v. Wade, 105
Rule of law
courts and, 25
deliberative democracy and, 57
executive power and, 18–19
freedom and, 2
legislative power and, 13–15
Thayerism and, 153n90
Waldron on, 153n90

Safety
absolutism and, 82
consumer, 60
environmental, 89, 107
highway, 21, 23, 45–46, 62, 90
occupational, 9, 48
statistical life and, 90
Same-sex marriage, 101
Scandal, 38
Schechter Poultry v. United States, 60, 67
Schmidt, Carl
Hamilton and, 15
legal issues and, 1–2, 6, 17, 20–21
liberalism and, 1–2
Nazis and, 1–3, 6, 15, 17, 20–21,
28
School prayer, 108
Second Amendment, 106
Securities and Exchange Commission
(SEC), 59–60, 62, 64, 67, 71
SEC v. Jarkesy, 59, 67, 71
Segregation, 102, 106, 108, 120,
152n70
Seila Law, 64–66, 74, 138n16
Self-government
deliberative democracy and, 22
executive power and, 22, 25
Madison and, 3
Thayerism and, 105
U.S. Constitution and, 2–3, 25, 105
Senate
Article I and, 3
bicameralism and, 21, 68
confirmation by, 47–48
deliberative democracy and, 50
impeachment and, 6, 133n9
judicial power and, 6
OIRA and, 47–48
partyism and, 124
reelection and, 47
*Separation-of-Powers Counterrevolution,
The* (Bowie and Renan), 133n12
Seventh Amendment, 67, 138n22

Sexual issues
    abortion, 100–102, 106, 108
    affirmative action, 100–101, 105–108
    birth control, 103
    discrimination, 99, 106, 108
    explicit speech, 13
    marriage, 101, 103, 115
    partyism, 113, 117–118
    Roe v. Wade, 105
    same-sex marriage, 101
Socialism, 118
Social media, 39, 120
Social Security Administration, 9, 20, 24
Sood, Gaurav, 155n40
Sovereignty
    freedom and, 2
    Grand Narrative and, 69
    immunity and, 69
    liberty and, 2
    major questions doctrine and, 85
    nondelegation doctrine and, 80–81
    one-party rule, 121, 124
    Thayerism and, 96
    U.S. Constitution and, 2, 96
Stalin, Joseph, 2
Statistical life, 90
Stem cell research, 123

Take Care Clause, 18, 63–64
Talking points, 39, 47
Taxes
    IRS and, 10
    legislative power and, 7
    major questions doctrine and, 87
    nondelegation doctrine and, 81
    partyism and, 122
    Thayerism and, 104
Tenure, 19
Terrorism, 122
Textualism
    freedom and, 4
    major questions doctrine and, 87–88,
        91–93, 146n32

    religion and, 153n91
    Thayerism and, 99–101, 104
Thayerism
    amendments and, 6, 100, 102, 104
    as arms control, 95, 110–111
    Bickel and, 101, 103–104, 151n73
    Calabresi on, 152n79
    conservatism and, 106–107
    contemporary context of, 107–109
    criminal law and, 103
    discretion and, 101
    Due Process Clause and, 100, 102,
        106, 108
    elections and, 103
    Ely and, 103–105
    Equal Protection Clause and, 8, 100,
        106
    executive power and, 96, 99
    experts and, 108, 152n79
    failure to adopt, 105
    Frankfurter and, 98–103, 109, 151n59
    freedom and, 109
    free foot of, 73, 96–97
    Grand Narrative and, 73–74
    Hand and, 98, 109, 150n33
    independence and, 96
    information and, 104
    interpretation and, 95–101, 104,
        145n8, 146n22
    judicial power and, 73, 95–111
    labor and, 102
    legal issues and, 98, 101–102, 108
    legislative power and, 95–104,
        107–110
    liberalism and, 106–107
    liberty and, 98
    limited role of courts and, 73, 95, 98,
        103
    neutrality and, 101–103
    New Deal and, 102
    Origin and Scope of the American
        Doctrine of Constitutional Law, The,
        149n1

popular constitutionalism and, 107

public health and, 107

public meaning originalists and, 100, 106, 152n79

reasonable doubt and, 73, 95–101, 104–106

reform and, 98

regulation and, 99–102, 107

relevance and, 109–110

religion and, 104, 108–109, 153n91

Republicans and, 105

rule of law and, 153n90

scope of, 98–99

self-government and, 105

sovereignty and, 96

taxes and, 104

textualism and, 99–101, 104

tradition and, 102

Trump and, 94

U.S. Constitution and, 95–111

Thermometer ratings, 114

Thomas, Clarence, 67

Tradition

deliberative democracy and, 49

executive power and, 7, 19–20

freedom and, 5

Grand Narrative and, 61, 70, 72, 137–138n10

judicial power and, 23

legislative power and, 7, 10–11, 14

liberal, 3

major questions doctrine and, 92–93

Thayerism and, 102

Trump, Donald

courts and, 27–36, 135n3, 136n24

deep state and, 38

deliberative democracy and, 51, 54–55

Grand Narrative and, 65

immunity and, 27–36

judicial power and, 27–33, 65, 94, 135n3, 136n24

partyism and, 113, 125

Thayerism and, 94

Trump v. Anderson, 35–36

Trump v. United States

brief opinion of, 28–29

criminal law and, 27, 30–34, 36

immunity and, 27–36

Jackson and, 28–29, 34

new framework of, 27

United States v. Klein and, 29–30

unquestionable power and, 27–28

unreviewability and, 29

Trust game, 116

Tyranny

courts and, 24–25

executive power and, 128

freedom and, 2–3

Madison and, 24

partyism and, 128

preventing, 2–3

Unemployment, 127

Unions, 46–47, 138n23, 144n19, 148n62

Unitary executive, 63–65

United States v. Carolene Products, 104

United States v. Klein, 29–30

Unreviewability, 29

U.S. Constitution

amendments to, 13, 67, 100, 102, 104, 106, 138n22, 143n11

articles of, 3 (*see also specific article*)

Bill of Rights, 2, 152n79

checks and balances of, 5–6, 152n79

courts and, 24–25

deliberative democracy and, 3, 56

democratic disorder and, 35

Due Process Clause, 79–80, 100, 102, 106, 108, 143n11

Equal Protection Clause, 8, 100, 106

executive power and, 18–19

Ex Post Facto Clause, 79–80

fourth branch of Government and, 59–60, 69

freedom and, 2–6

U.S. Constitution (cont.)
Grand Narrative and, 59–74
Hamilton and, 11–15
immunity and, 27–36
independence and, 11–12, 14, 60–66,
96, 99, 101, 106, 110, 128, 142n92
interpretation of, 4–5, 11–15, 25,
66, 72–74, 79–80, 87, 93–101,
104, 106, 128, 132n21, 141n85,
142n92, 146n39
legislative power and, 11–15
as liberal document, 2
liberty and, 2, 15, 25, 78–79, 98
Madison and, 3, 66, 96, 152n79
major questions doctrine and, 85, 87–
88, 91–93
nondelegation doctrine and, 78–83
pardons and, 31
prenumbral, 82
reasonable doubt and, 73, 95–101,
104–105
reprieves and, 31
self-government and, 2–3, 25, 105
sovereignty and, 2, 96
Take Care Clause, 18, 63–64
Thayerism and, 95–111
Usery v. Turner Elkhorn Mining, 143n11
U.S. Supreme Court
*AFL-CIO v. American Petroleum
Institute*, 138n23, 144n19, 148n62
*Alabama Association of Realtors v.
Department of Health & Human
Services*, 148n71
Alito, 68, 72
American Trucking, 62, 74
*Ameron, Inc. v. Army Corps of
Engineers*, 137–138n10
Barrett, 86–94, 148n71
Biden v. Nebraska, 93
Black, 102
Bolling v. Sharpe, 98, 102–103
*Bowen v. Georgetown University
Hospital*, 134n22, 143n1

Brandeis, 99, 101, 109
Breyer, 106
Brown v. Board of Education, 102–103
Bush v. Gore, 35
Cardozo, 109
Chevron v. NRDC, 66, 74
Citizens United v. FEC, 98
Clinton v. Jones, 135n2
Crowell v. Benson, 20, 61–62, 66–67,
71, 74
democratic disorder and, 35
Douglas, 102–103
EEOC v. Arabian American Oil Co.,
134n23
Erie case, 23
*FDA v. Brown & Williamson Tobacco
Corp.*, 93, 144n1, 148n64
Frankfurter, 98–99, 101–103, 109,
151n59
Free Enterprise Fund, 63–64
FTC v. Ruberoid Co., 59, 137–138n10
Gorsuch, 67–71, 85–88, 91–94,
145n8, 146n39, 148n71
Gundy v. United States, 68
Harlan, 103
Holmes, 95, 99, 101–102, 109
Humphrey's Executor v. United States,
61–65, 74, 139n39, 139n42
immunity and, 27–36
INS v. Chadha, 63
Jackson, 7–8, 28–29, 34, 59
judicial power and, 3
Kagan, 147n41
Kent v. Dulles, 148n60
Lochner v. New York, 97, 102
Loper Bright Enterprises v. Raimondo,
66, 138n16, 139n46, 139n48
Marbury v. Madison, 66, 96, 133n10
Marshall, 66, 96
McCulloch v. Maryland, 142n96
MCI, 88, 93, 146n32
*Michigan Citizens for an Independent
Press v. Thornburg*, 144n17

Muscogee (Creek) Nation v. Hodel,
    143n2
Myers v. United States, 64
popular constitutionalism and, 107
pragmatism and, 73–74
Roberts, 67, 138n10, 138n16
Roe v. Wade, 105
Schechter Poultry v. United States, 60,
    67
SEC v. Jarkesy, 59, 67, 71
Seila Law, 64–66, 74, 138n16
Thomas, 67
Trump v. Anderson, 35–36
Trump v. United States, 27–36
United States v. Carolene Products, 104
United States v. Klein, 29–30
unreviewability and, 29
Usery v. Turner Elkhorn Mining, 143n11
Warren, 104
West Virginia v. EPA, 68
*Youngstown Sheet & Steel Tube Co. v.
    Sawyer*, 21, 28, 30

Vesting Clause, 69, 85
Violence, 1, 128

Waldron, Jeremy, 153n90
Warren, Earl, 104
Weapons of mass destruction (WMD),
    122
Welfare, 106, 114, 142n96
West Virginia v. EPA, 68
Westwood, Sean, 115–116, 120, 154n9
White House, 9
    deliberative democracy and, 50,
        54–55
    election fraud and, 33
    immunity and, 33
    OIRA and, 8, 47–48
    partyism and, 124
Wittgenstein, Ludwig
    Barrett and, 86, 90–93, 148n71
    communication and, 86, 88

games and, 86
major questions doctrine and, 86–93,
    148n71

*Youngstown Sheet & Steel Tube Co. v.
    Sawyer*, 21, 28, 30